KEVIN McCOLLUM   JEFFREY SELLER   JILL FURMAN
SANDER JACOBS   GOODMAN/GROSSMAN   PETER FINE   EVERETT/SKIPPER

PRESENT

IN THE **** HEIGHTS
A New Musical

MUSIC AND LYRICS BY
LIN-MANUEL MIRANDA

BOOK BY
QUIARA ALEGRÍA HUDES

CONCEIVED BY
LIN-MANUEL MIRANDA

WITH

ANDRÉA BURNS   JANET DACAL   ROBIN DE JESÚS   CARLOS GOMEZ
MANDY GONZALEZ   CHRISTOPHER JACKSON   PRISCILLA LOPEZ   OLGA MEREDIZ
LIN-MANUEL MIRANDA   KAREN OLIVO   SETH STEWART

AND

TONY CHIROLDES   ROSIE LANI FIEDELMAN   JOSHUA HENRY   AFRA HINES
NINA LAFARGA   DOREEN MONTALVO   JAVIER MUÑOZ   KRYSTA RODRIGUEZ
ELISEO ROMÁN   LUIS SALGADO   SHAUN TAYLOR-CORBETT   RICKEY TRIPP
MICHAEL BALDERRAMA   BLANCA CAMACHO   ROGELIO DOUGLAS JR.   STEPHANIE KLEMONS

SET DESIGN	COSTUME DESIGN	LIGHTING DESIGN	SOUND DESIGN
ANNA LOUIZOS	PAUL TAZEWELL	HOWELL BINKLEY	ACME SOUND PARTNERS

ARRANGEMENTS & ORCHESTRATIONS
ALEX LACAMOIRE & BILL SHERMAN

MUSIC COORDINATOR
MICHAEL KELLER

CASTING	PRESS REPRESENTATIVE	MARKETING	COMPANY MANAGER
TELSEY + COMPANY	BARLOW·HARTMAN	SCOTT A. MOORE	BRIG BERNEY

GENERAL MANAGEMENT	TECHNICAL SUPERVISOR	PRODUCTION STAGE MANAGER	ASSOCIATE PRODUCERS
JOHN S. CORKER LIZBETH CONE	BRIAN LYNCH	J. PHILIP BASSETT	RUTH HENDEL HAROLD NEWMAN

MUSIC DIRECTION BY
ALEX LACAMOIRE

CHOREOGRAPHED BY
ANDY BLANKENBUEHLER

DIRECTED BY
THOMAS KAIL

DEVELOPMENT OF *IN THE HEIGHTS* WAS SUPPORTED BY THE EUGENE O'NEILL THEATER CENTER
DURING A RESIDENCY AT THE MUSIC THEATER CONFERENCE OF 2005.

INITIALLY DEVELOPED BY BACK HOUSE PRODUCTIONS.

Opening Night March 9, 2008

www.intheheightsthemusical.com
Cover photos by Vincent Dixon. Courtesy of SpotCo.

*The composer would like to thank especially Alex Lacamoire and Bill Sherman
for their effort and assistance in preparing this book.*

ISBN 978-1-4234-4581-4

WILLIAMSON MUSIC®
A RODGERS AND HAMMERSTEIN COMPANY
www.williamsonmusic.com

EXCLUSIVELY DISTRIBUTED BY

HAL·LEONARD®
CORPORATION

7777 W. BLUEMOUND RD. P.O. BOX 13819 MILWAUKEE, WI 53213

Visit Hal Leonard Online at
www.halleonard.com

LIN-MANUEL MIRANDA

is the star-composer-lyricist of Broadway's 2008 Tony® Award Winner for Best Musical, *In the Heights. In the Heights* received 4 Tony® Awards, including Best Original Score for Lin-Manuel, who also received a Tony® nomination for Best Leading Actor in a Musical. Off Broadway, the show received 9 Drama Desk nominations, including Best Music and Best Lyrics, and won the award for Outstanding Ensemble Performance. Additionally, *In the Heights* won the Lucille Lortel Award and Outer Critic's Circle Award for Best Musical. Lin-Manuel received an Obie Award for Outstanding Music and Lyrics for the show.

As an actor, Lin-Manuel received a 2007 Theater World Award for Outstanding Debut Performance and the 2007 Clarence Derwent Award for Most Promising Male Performance, courtesy of Actor's Equity Foundation. Lin-Manuel also received the ASCAP Foundation's Richard Rodgers New Horizons Award at its annual ceremony in December of 2007 and a Medal of Honor from the National Arts Club in 2008.

Lin-Manuel is a co-founder and member of Freestyle Love Supreme, a popular hip-hop improv group that performs regularly in New York City. The group has also toured the Edinburgh Fringe Festival, as well as the Aspen, Melbourne and Montreal Comedy Festivals. He lives in New York.

I used to dream about this moment, now I'm in it.
Tell the conductor to hold the baton a minute
I'll start with Alex Lacamoire and Bill Sherman
Kevin McCollum, Jeffrey Seller and Jill Furman
Quiara for keeping the pages turning
Tommy Kail for keeping the engine burnin'
For bein' so discernin' through every all nighter
Dr. Herbert for tellin' me, "you're a writer"
I have to thank Andy Blank for every spank
Matter fact, thank John Buzzetti for every drink
Thank the cast and crew for having each other's backs, son
I don't know about God but I believe in Chris Jackson
I don't know what else I got, I'm off the dome
I know I wrote a little show about home
Mr. Sondheim, look, I made a hat
Where there never was a hat!
It's a Latin hat at that!
Mom, Dad and Cita, I wrote a play,
Y'all came to every play
Thanks for being here today
Vanessa, who still leaves me breathless
Thanks for lovin' me when I was broke and makin' breakfast
And with that, I want to thank all my Latino people
This is for Abuelo Wisin and Puerto Rico
Thank you.

—Lin-Manuel Miranda
Rap after receiving the 2008 Tony® Award
for Best Original Score

CONTENTS

IN THE HEIGHTS

Music and Lyrics by LIN-MANUEL MIRANDA
Arrangement by ALEX LACAMOIRE
and BILL SHERMAN

Hip-Hop, half-time feel

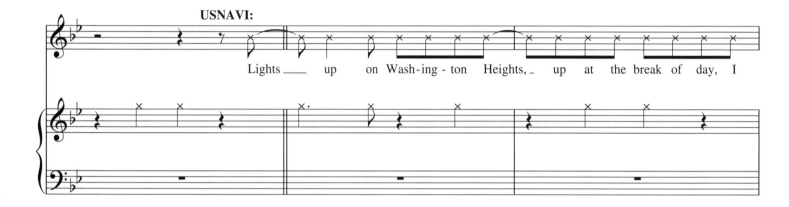

USNAVI:

Lights ___ up on Wash-ing-ton Heights, _ up at the break of day, I

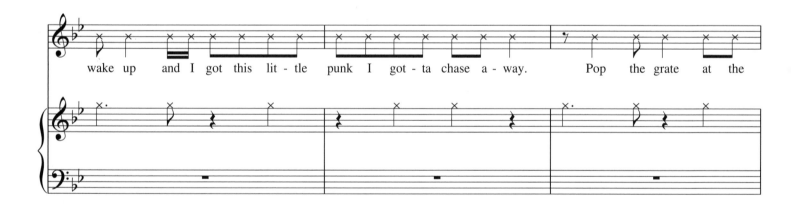

wake up and I got this lit-tle punk I got-ta chase a-way. Pop the grate at the

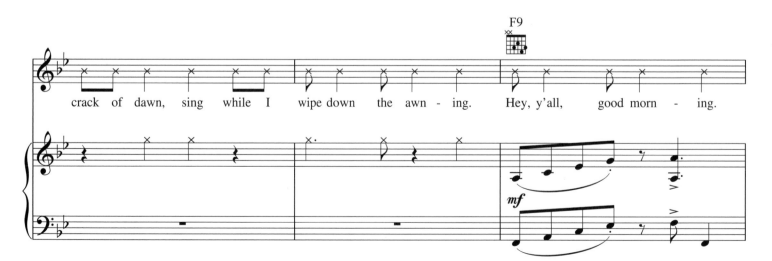

crack of dawn, sing while I wipe down the awn-ing. Hey, y'all, good morn-ing.

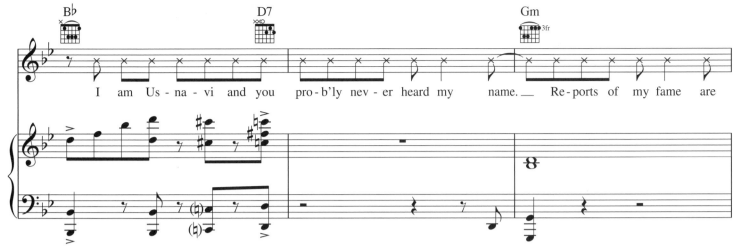

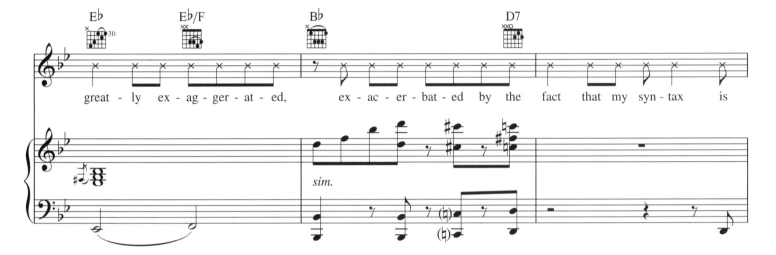

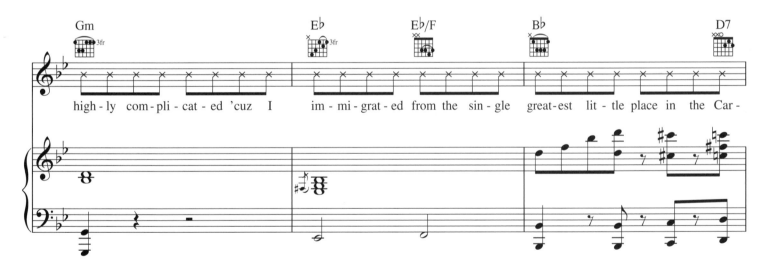

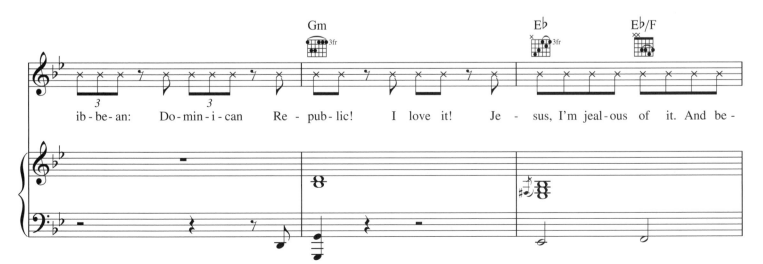

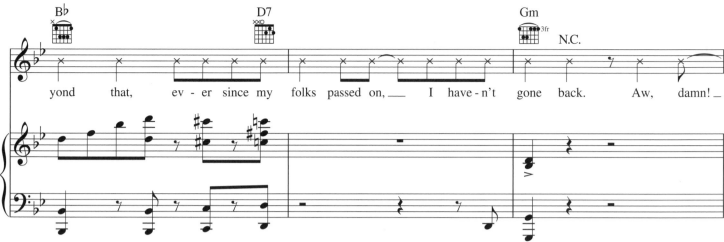

yond that, ev-er since my folks passed on, __ I have-n't gone back. Aw, damn! __

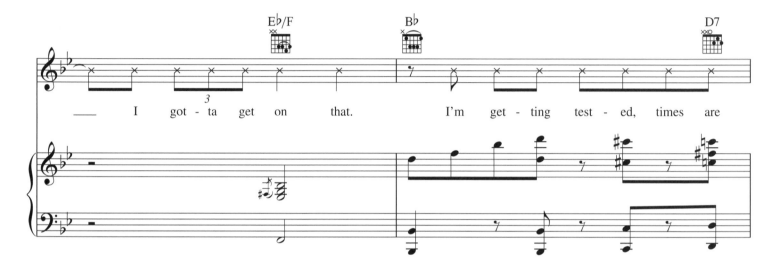

__ I got-ta get on that. I'm get-ting test-ed, times are

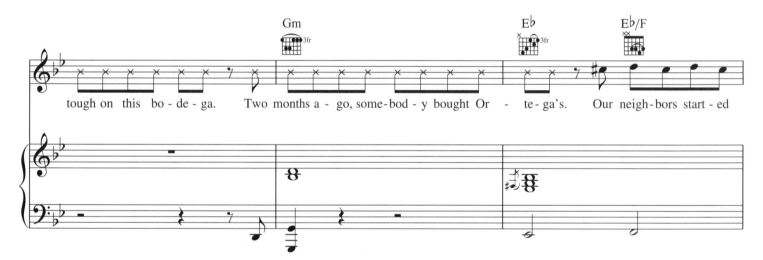

tough on this bo-de-ga. Two months a-go, some-bod-y bought Or-te-ga's. Our neigh-bors start-ed

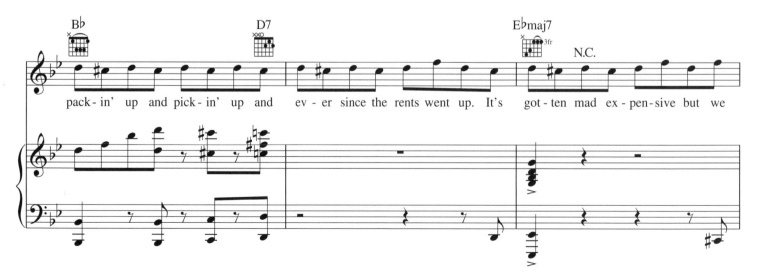

pack-in' up and pick-in' up and ev-er since the rents went up. It's got-ten mad ex-pen-sive but we

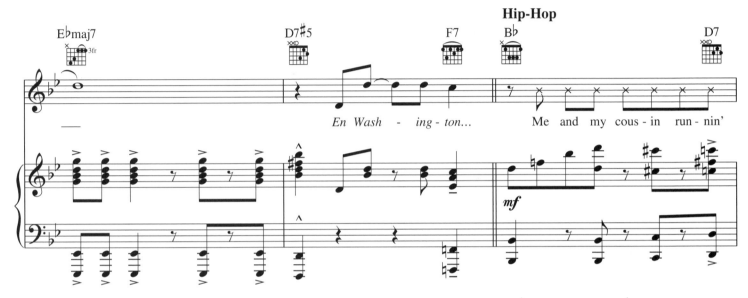

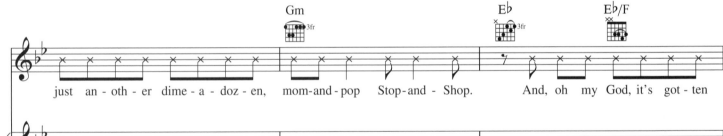

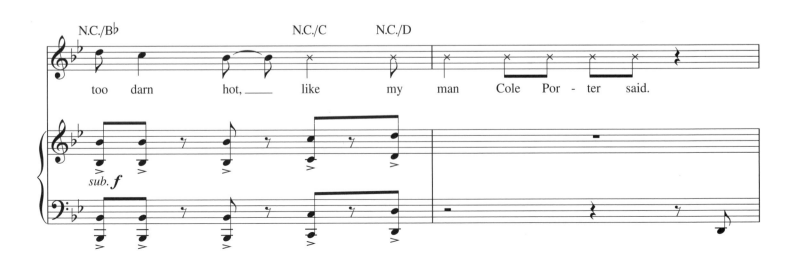

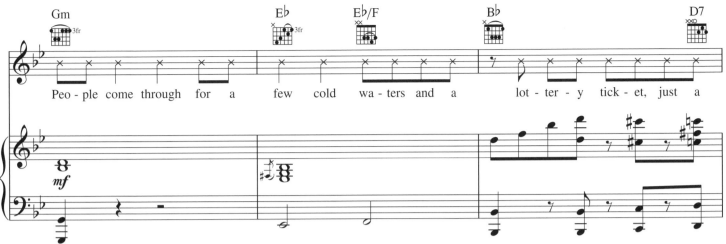

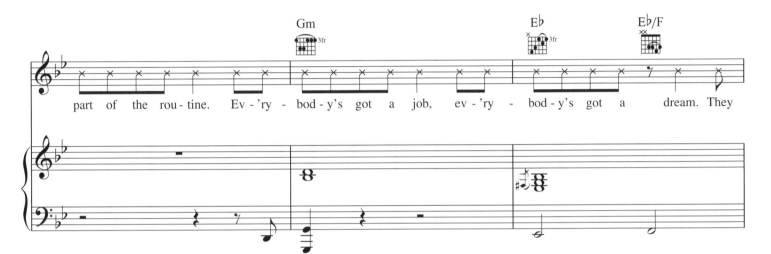

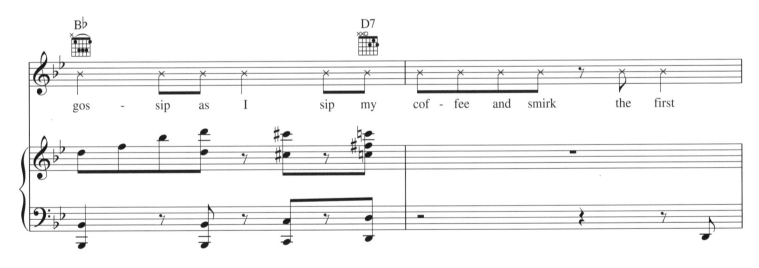

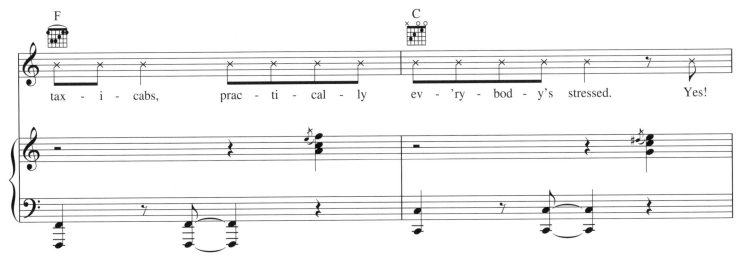

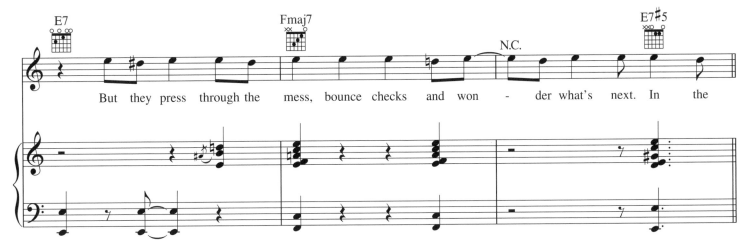

12

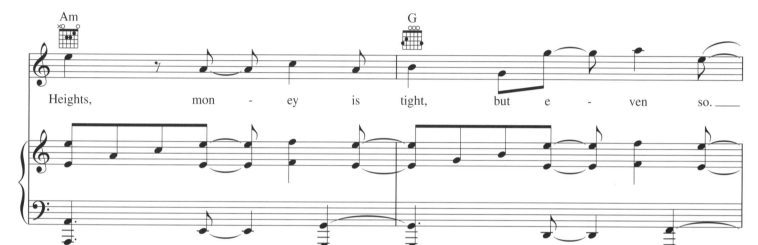

Hip-Hop

all a-bout the leg-a-cy they left with me, it's des-ti-ny. And one day I'll be on a beach with

Son-ny writ-ing checks to me.

COMMUNITY:

In the Heights, I ____ hang my flag up on ____ dis - play. ____

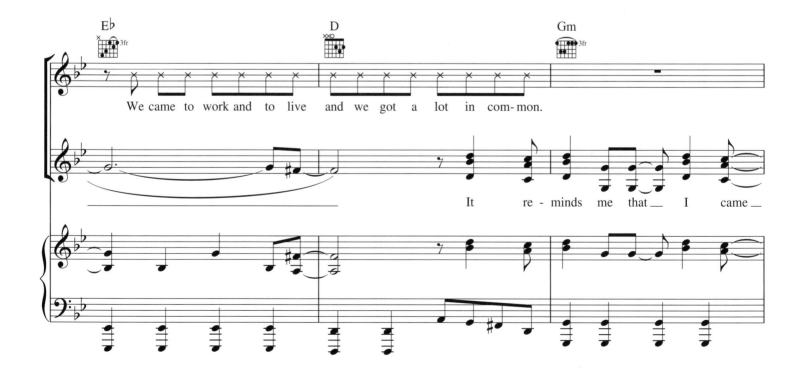

We came to work and to live and we got a lot in com-mon.

It re-minds me that ____ I came ____

15

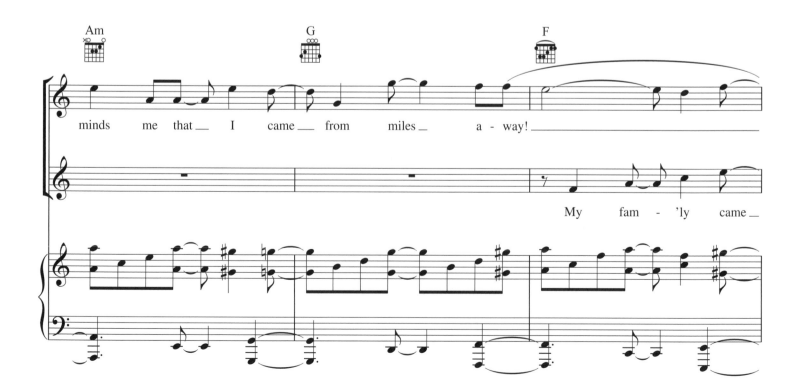

BREATHE

Music and Lyrics by LIN-MANUEL MIRANDA
Arrangement by ALEX LACAMOIRE
and BILL SHERMAN

Moderate Waltz

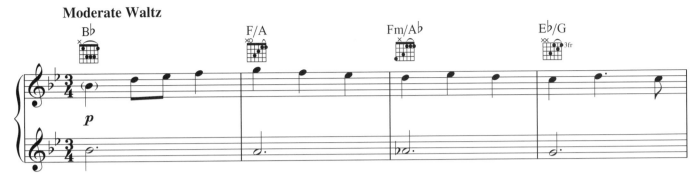

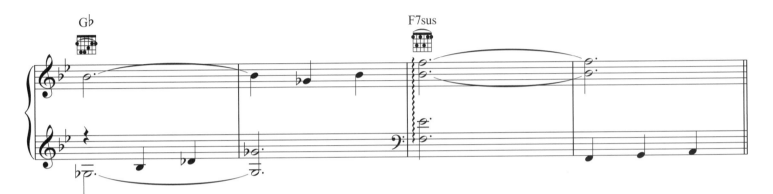

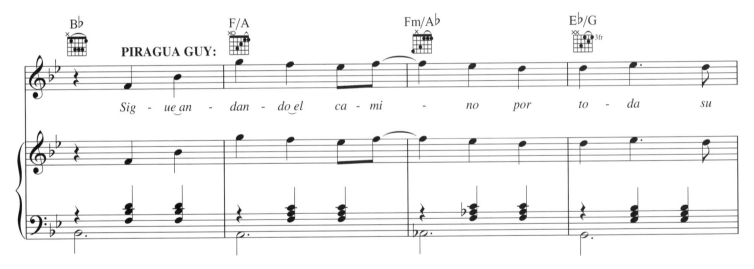

PIRAGUA GUY:

Si - gue an - dan - do el ca - mi - no por to - da su

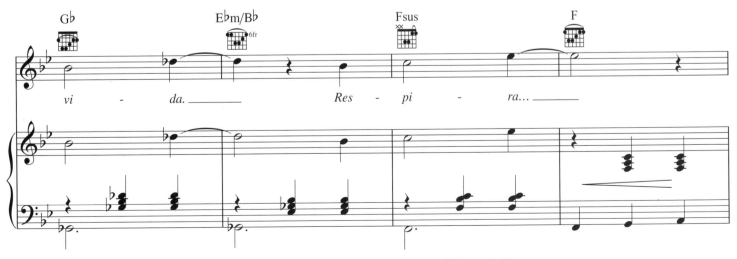

vi - da. Res - pi - ra...

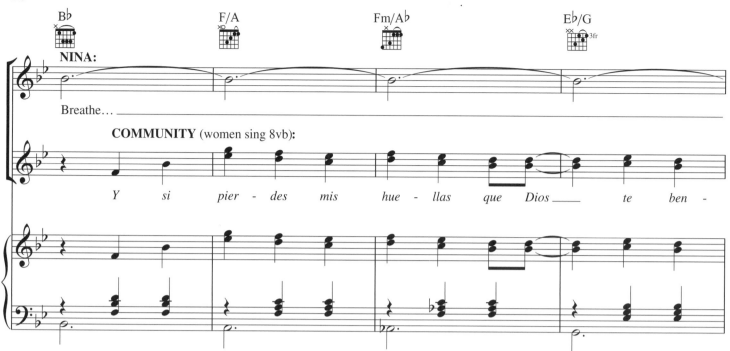

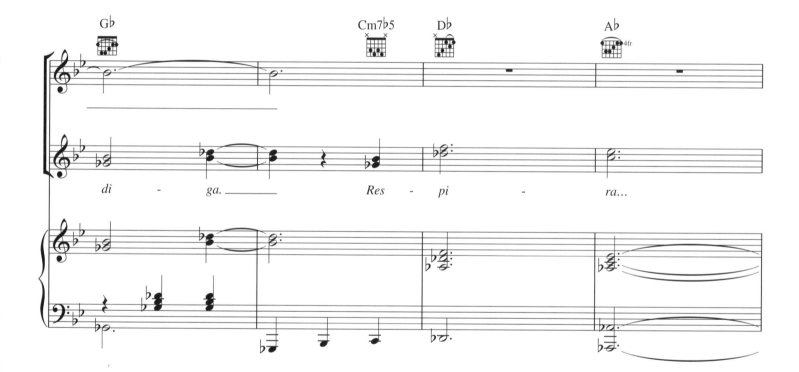

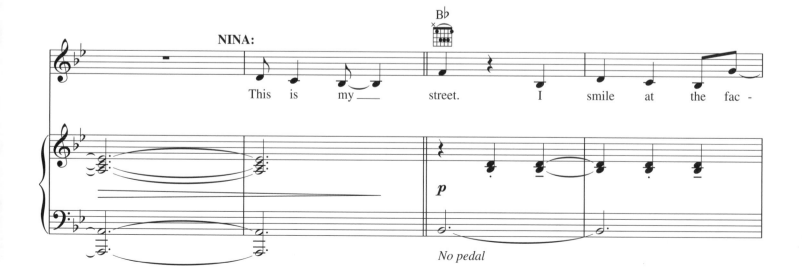

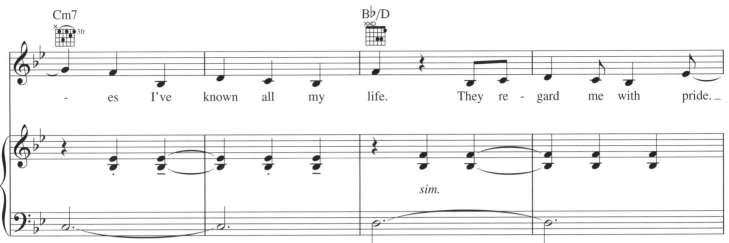

-es I've known all my life. They re-gard me with pride. _

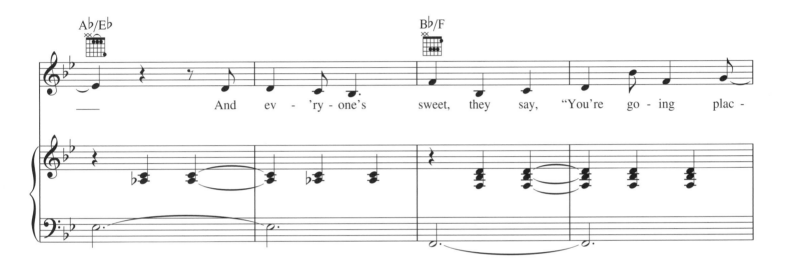

_ And ev-'ry-one's sweet, they say, "You're go-ing plac-

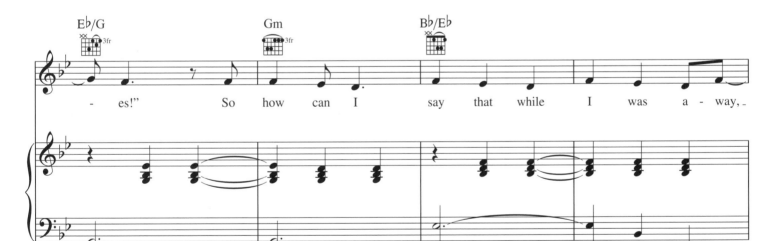

-es!" So how can I say that while I was a-way, _

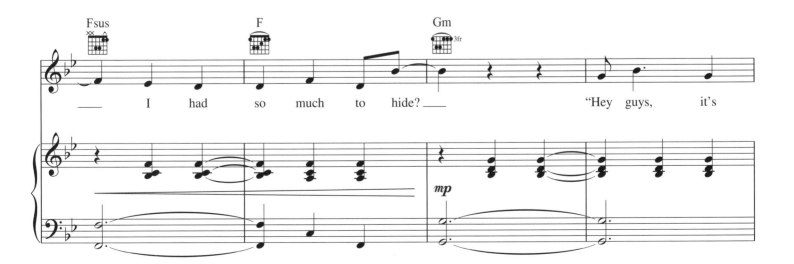

_ I had so much to hide? _ "Hey guys, it's

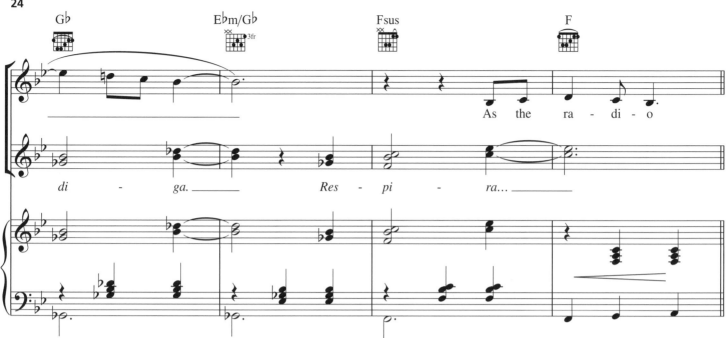

As the ra - di - o

di - ga._____ Res - pi - ra..._____

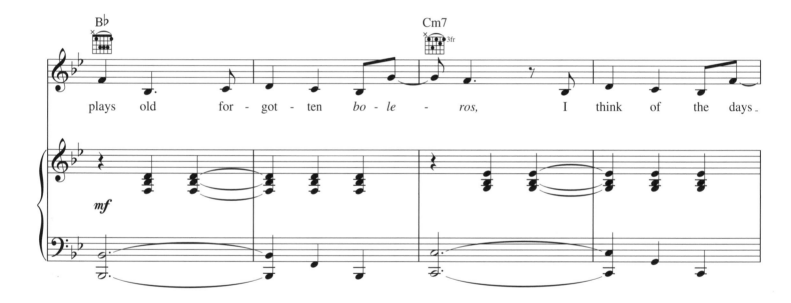

plays old for - got - ten *bo - le - ros,* I think of the days__

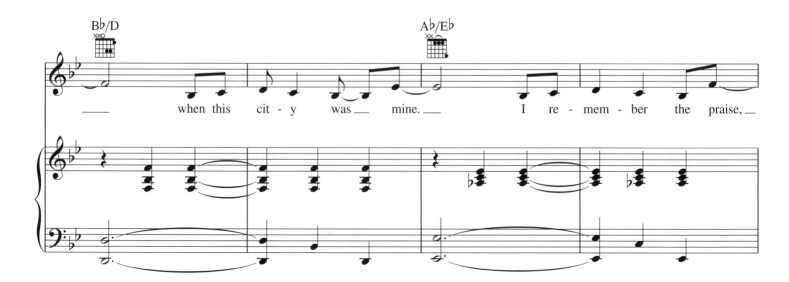

____ when this cit - y was__ mine.__ I re - mem - ber the praise,__

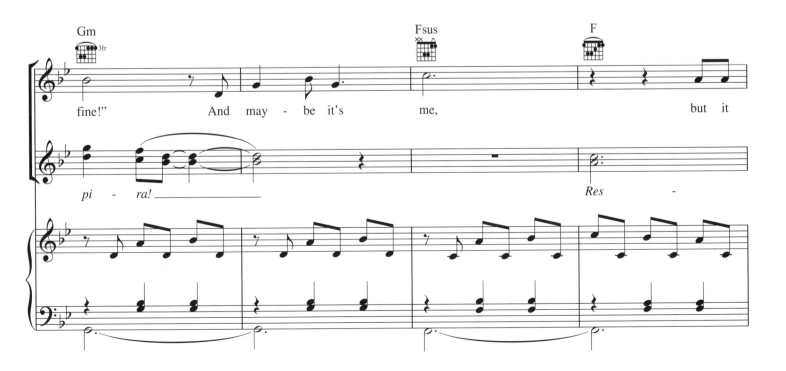

all seems like life - times a - go. _____ So

pi - *ra!* _____

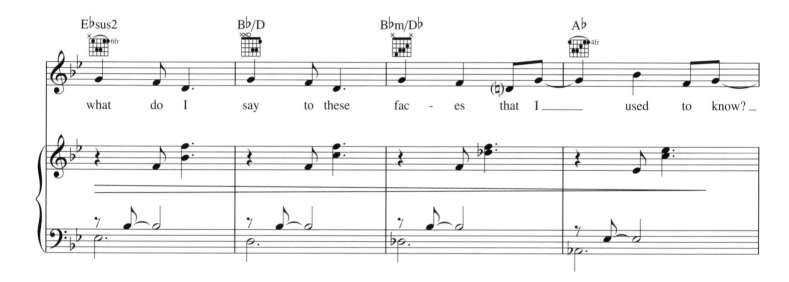

what do I say to these fac - es that I _____ used to know? _

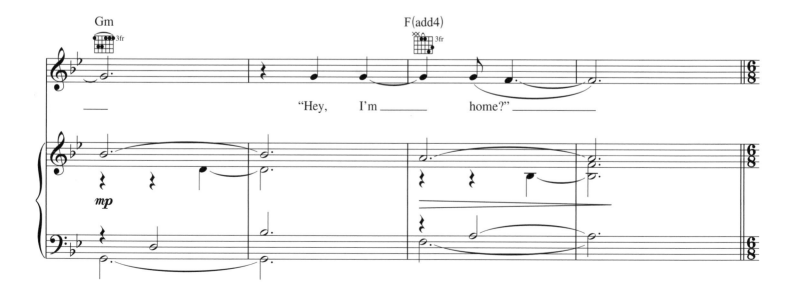

_____ "Hey, I'm _____ home?" _____

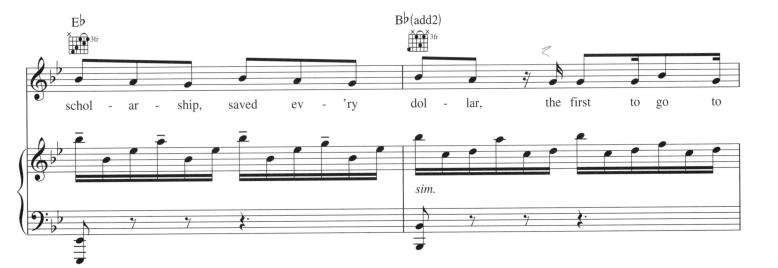

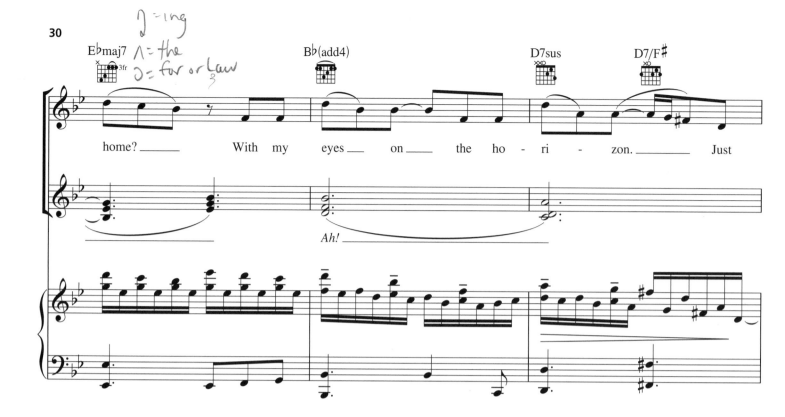

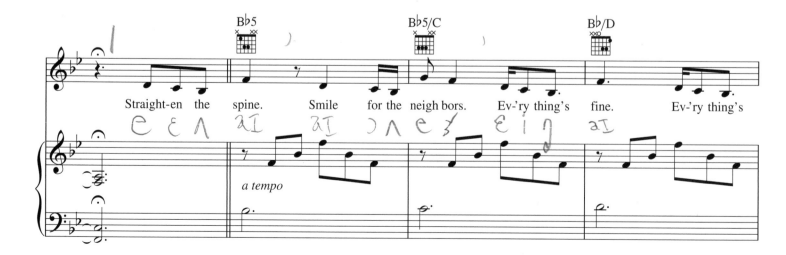

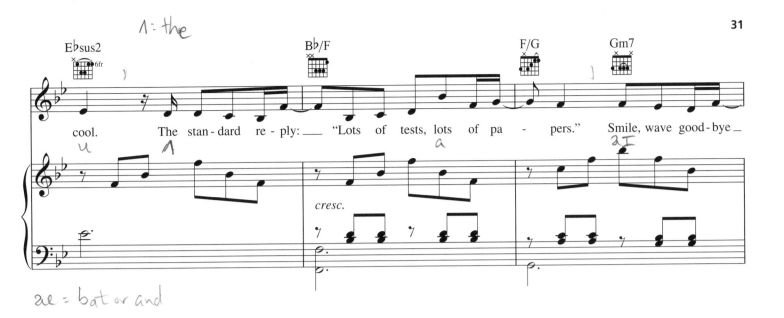

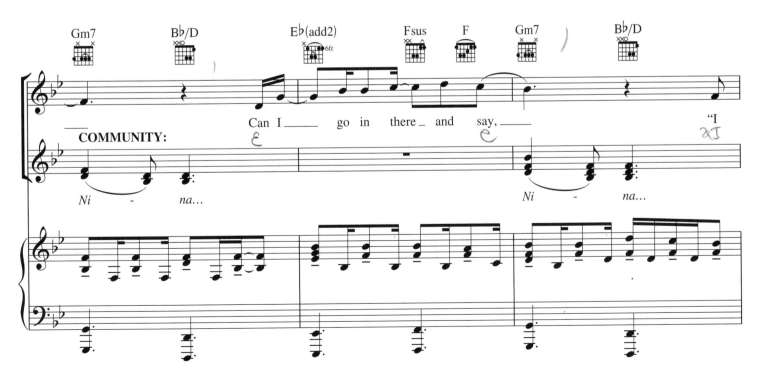

IT WON'T BE LONG NOW

Music and Lyrics by LIN-MANUEL MIRANDA
Arrangement by ALEX LACAMOIRE
and BILL SHERMAN

Allegro
N.C.

p

With pedal

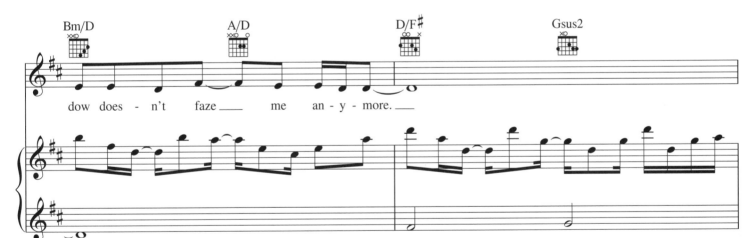

VANESSA:

The el-e-vat-ed train ___ by my win-

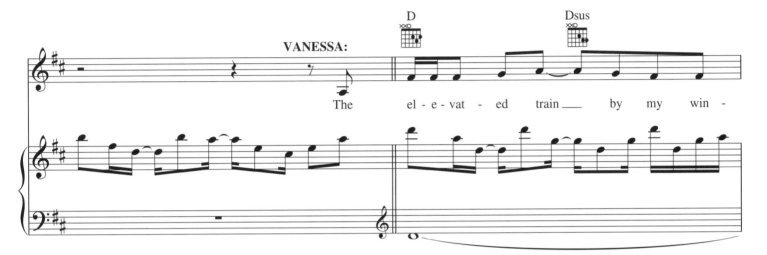

dow does-n't faze ___ me an-y-more. ___

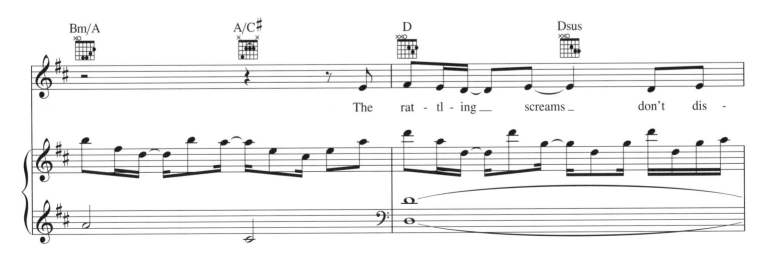

The rat-tl-ing ___ screams ___ don't dis-

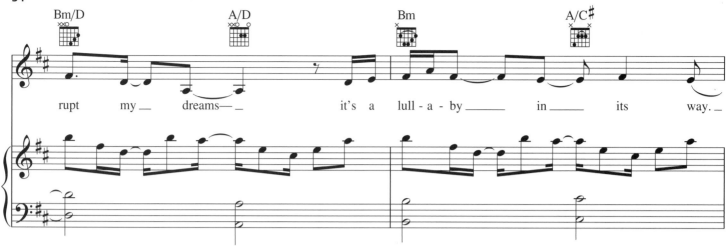

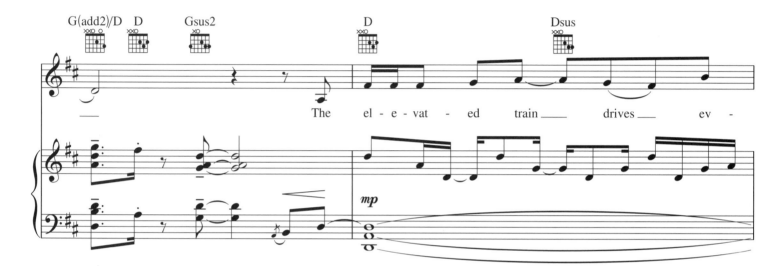

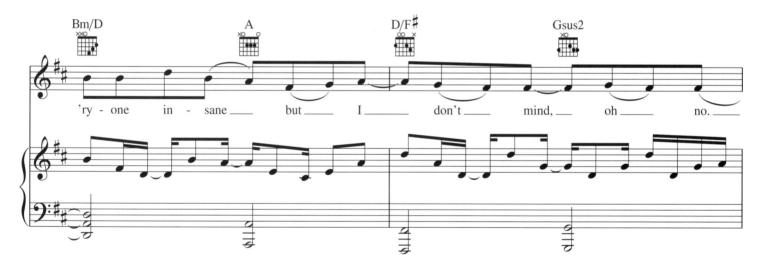

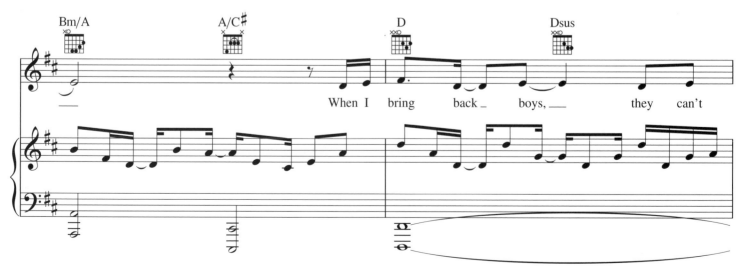

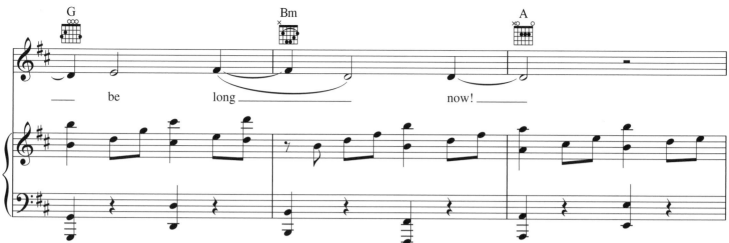

be long ____ now! ____

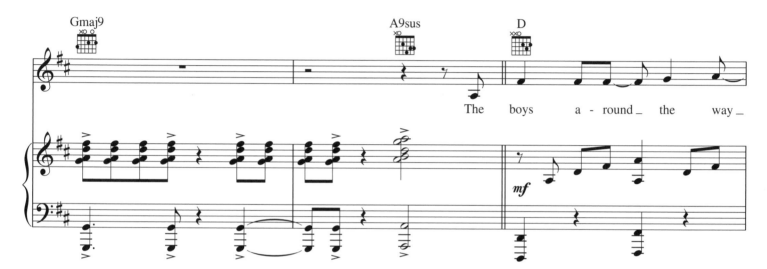

The boys a - round _ the way _

____ hol - ler at me when I'm walk - ing down the street. ____

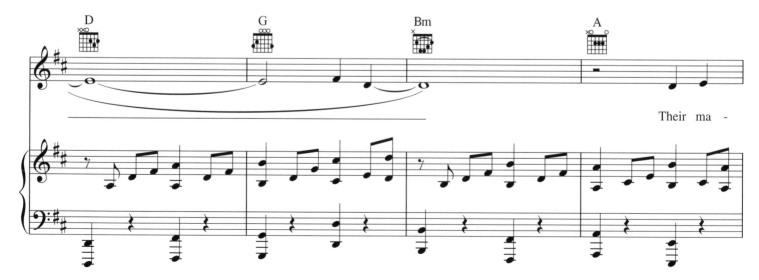

Their ma -

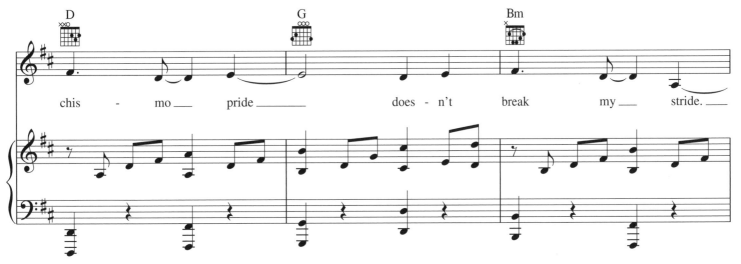

chis - mo ___ pride ___ does - n't break my ___ stride. ___

It's a com - pli - ment ___ so ___ they say. ___

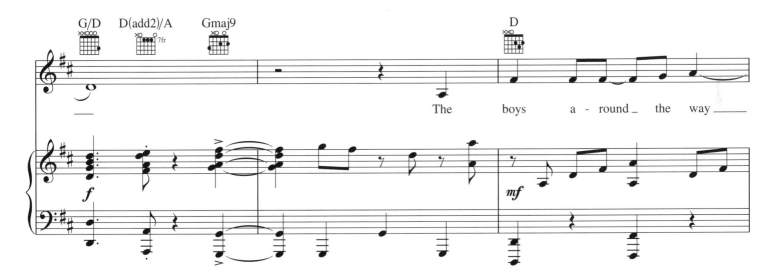

The boys a - round ___ the way ___

___ hol - ler at me ev - 'ry day, ___ but ___ I ___

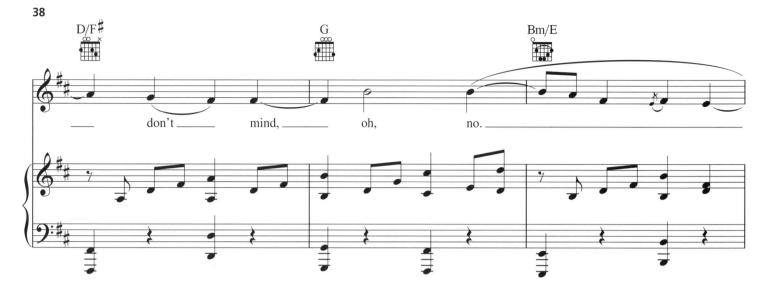

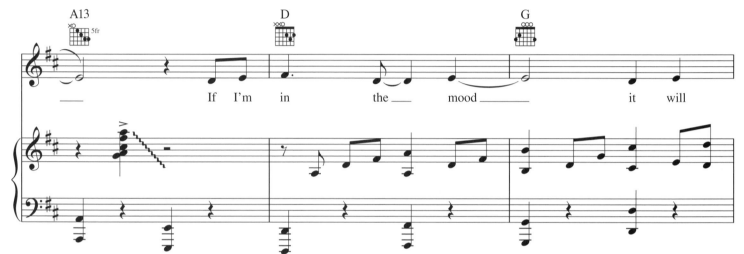

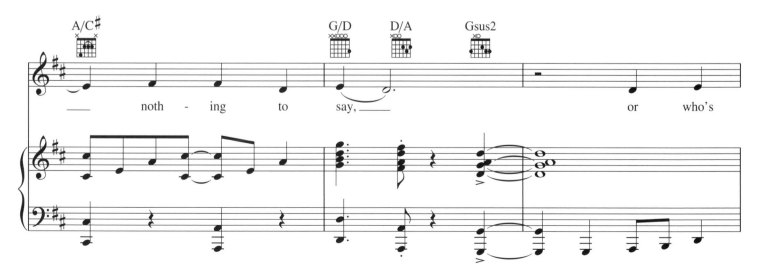

honk - ing at ___ me from ___ his Chev - ro - let! _____ One ___

day, I'm hop - pin' in a lim - ou - sine ____ and I'm driv -

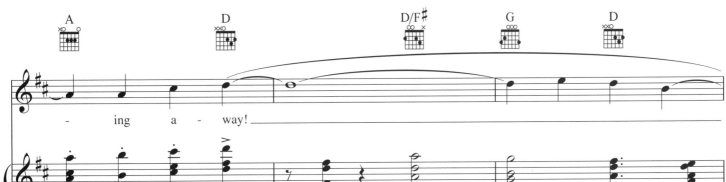

- ing a - way! _____

It won't ___

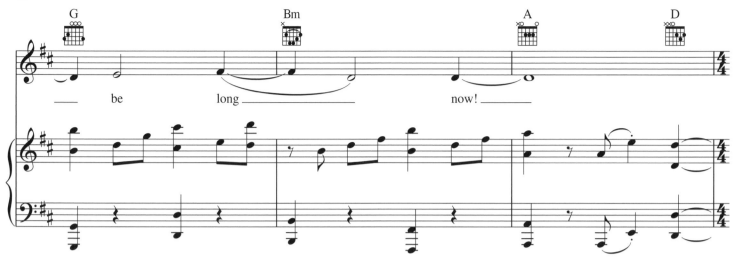

be long now!

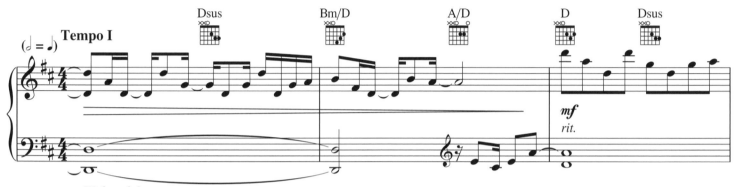

Tempo I ($\bullet = \bullet$)

With pedal

mf rit.

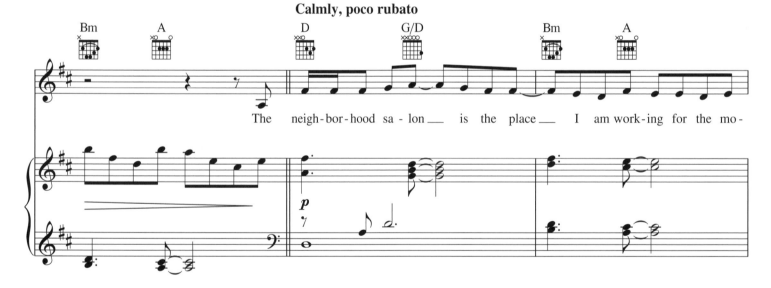

Calmly, poco rubato

The neigh-bor-hood sa-lon ___ is the place ___ I am work-ing for the mo-

p

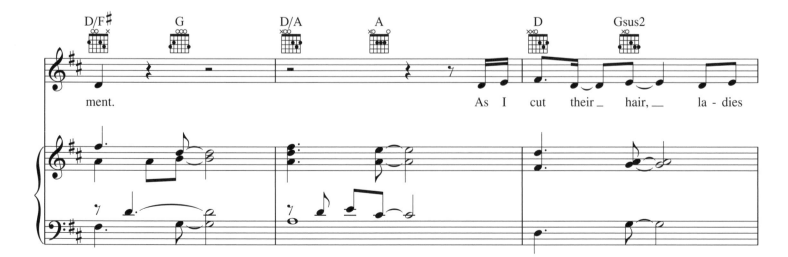

ment. As I cut their ___ hair, ___ la-dies

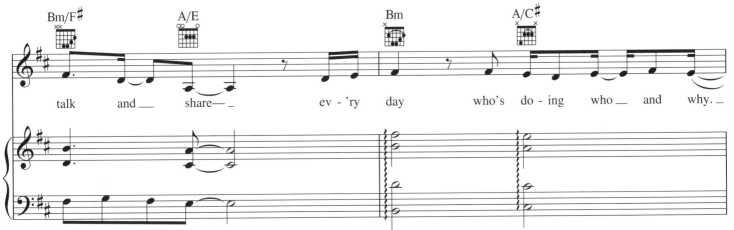

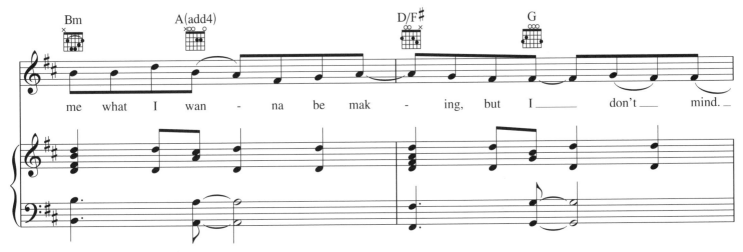

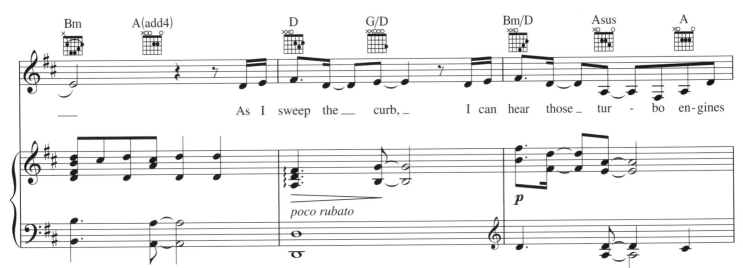

INÚTIL

Music and Lyrics by LIN-MANUEL MIRANDA
Arrangement by ALEX LACAMOIRE
and BILL SHERMAN

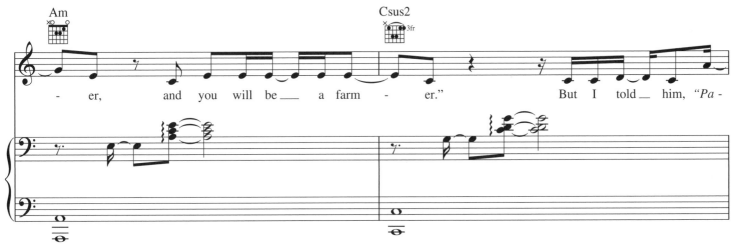

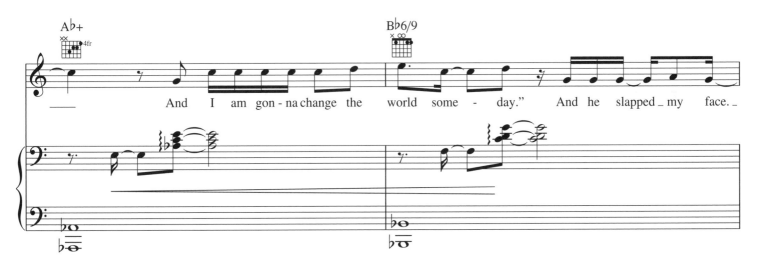

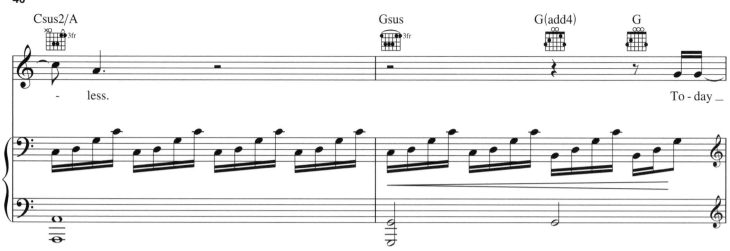

-less.	To-day __

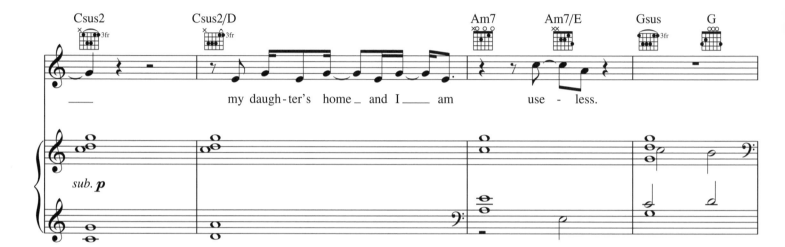

__	my daugh-ter's home __ and I __ am	use - less.

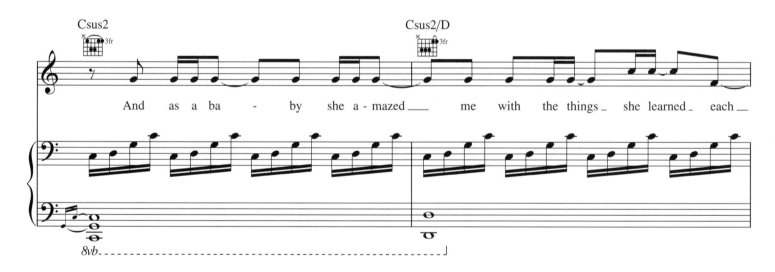

And	as a ba	- by she a-mazed ___ me	with	the things __ she learned __ each __

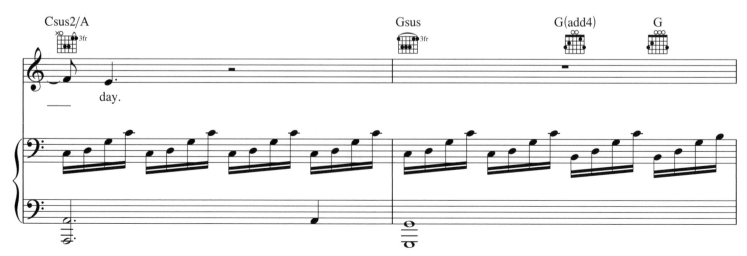

__	day.

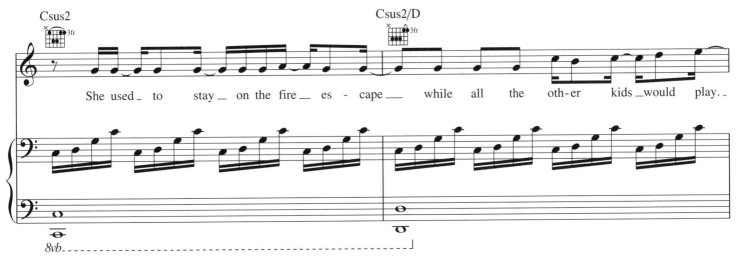

She used_ to stay_ on the fire_ es - cape__ while all the oth-er kids _would play. _

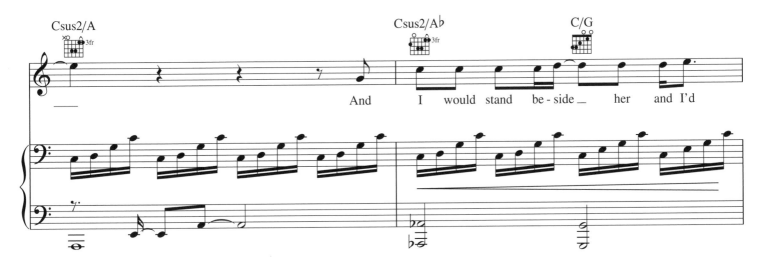

___ And I would stand be - side__ her and I'd

say: "I'm proud to be__ your fa - ther, 'cuz you work so__ much hard -

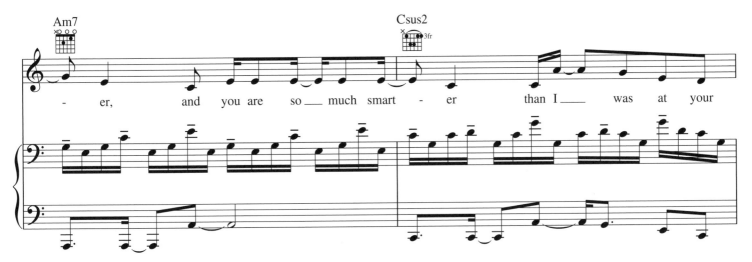

- er, and you are so__ much smart - er than I ___ was at your

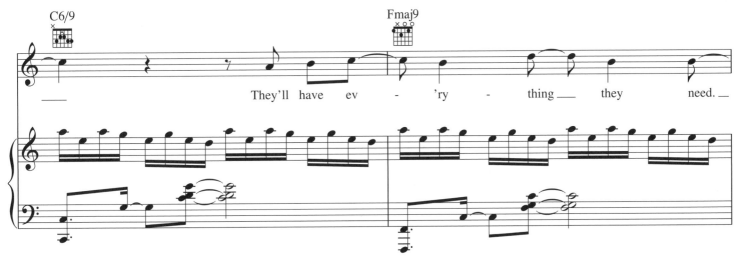

They'll have ev - 'ry - thing __ they need. __

Or all my work, __ all my life, __

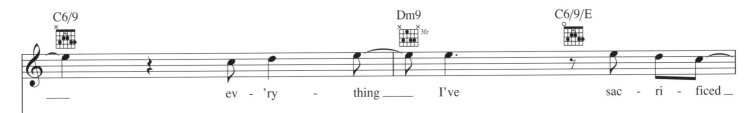

ev - 'ry - thing __ I've sac - ri - ficed __

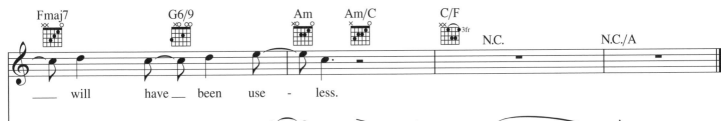

__ will have __ been use - less.

NO ME DIGA

Music and Lyrics by LIN-MANUEL MIRANDA
Arrangement by ALEX LACAMOIRE
and BILL SHERMAN

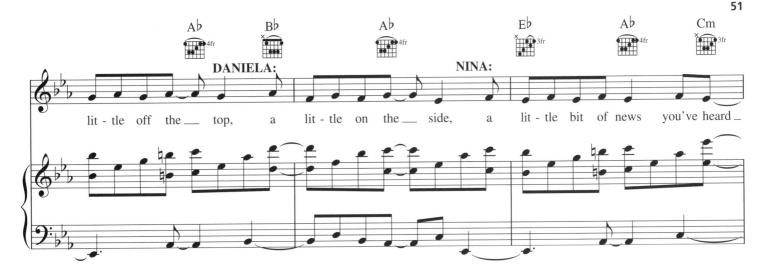

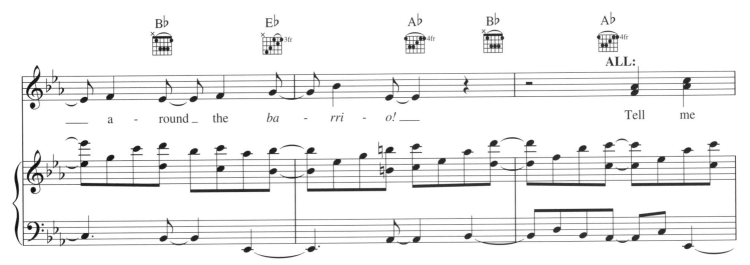

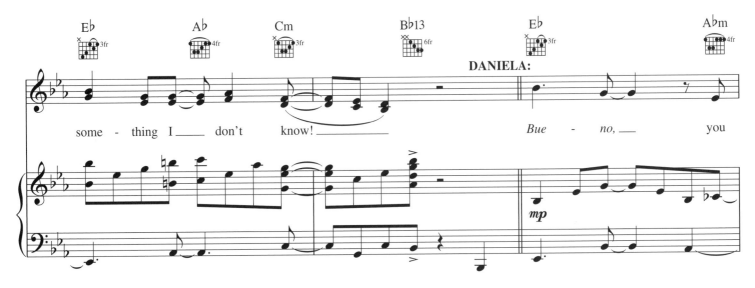

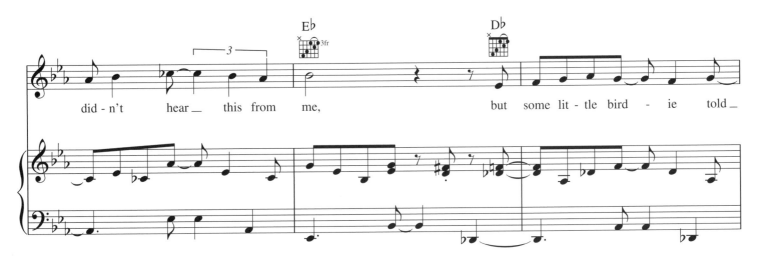

__ me, Us-na-vi had sex__ with Yo-lan-da!

VANESSA: Ay, no! He'd nev-er go out with a

CARLA & NINA: No me di-ga!

skank like that! __ Please tell me you're jok - ing! O-kay!

DANIELA: Just

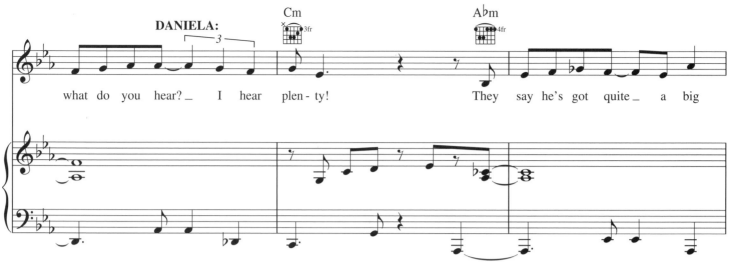

Bachata, l'istesso tempo

DANIELA:

Ni - na, se - ri - ous - ly, ___ ___ we knew ___ you'd be ___ the one ___ to make ___

___ it out! ___

VANESSA:

I'll bet ___ you im - pressed ___

___ them ___ all ___ out ___ west; ___ you were al - ways the best, ___ no doubt! ___

DANIELA/CARLA/VANESSA: *No me diga?!*
NINA: *I should go… (She exits)*
DANIELA: *That's a shitty piece of news.*
CARLA: *That girl never quit anything.*
VANESSA: *What the hell happened?*

Tempo I

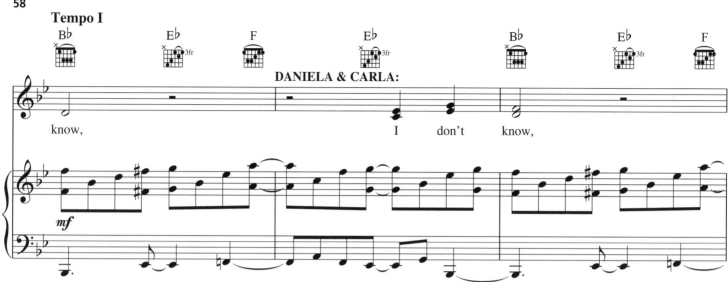

know,   DANIELA & CARLA: I   don't   know,

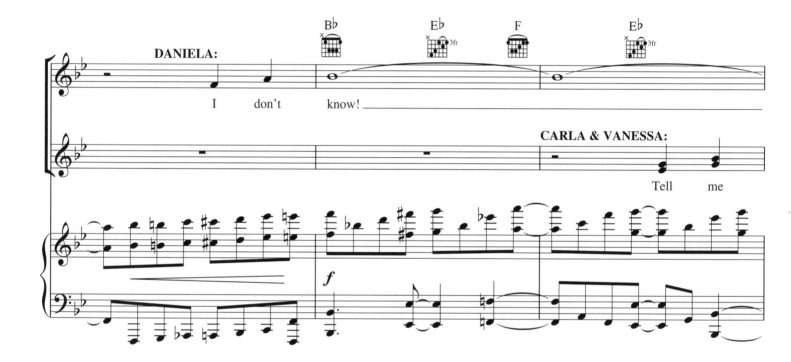

DANIELA: I   don't   know! _____

CARLA & VANESSA: Tell   me

some - thing I ____ don't   know! _____   *Qué sé yo?*

Qué sé yo?

96,000

Music and Lyrics by LIN-MANUEL MIRANDA
Arrangement by ALEX LACAMOIRE
and BILL SHERMAN

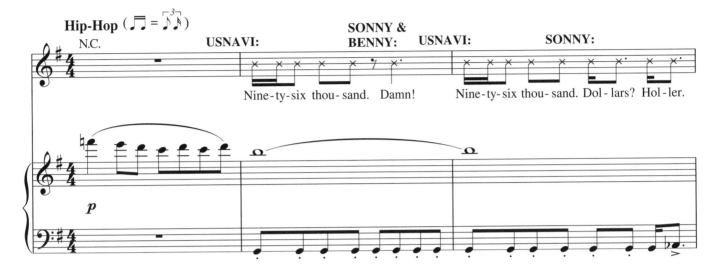

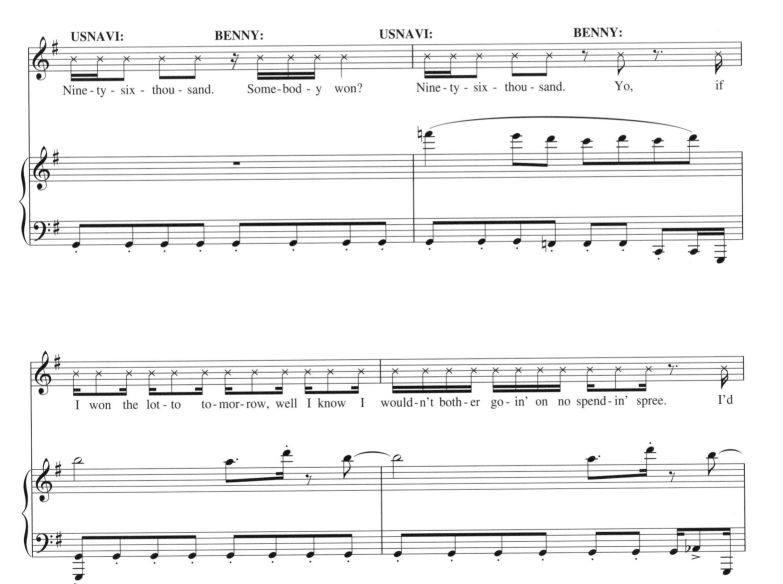

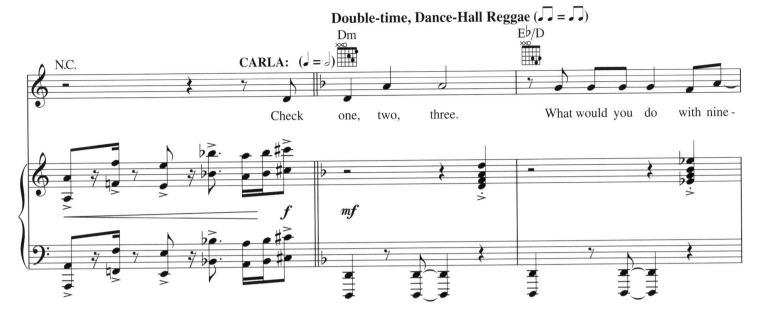

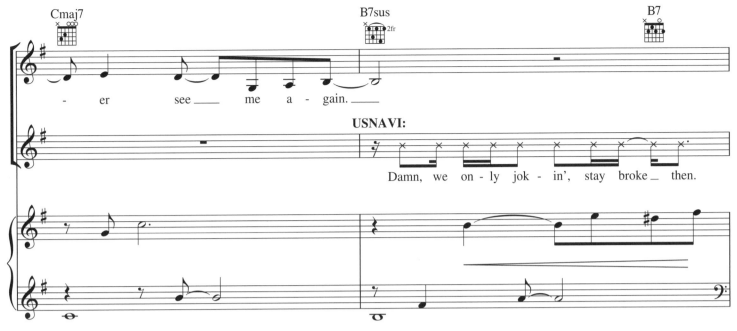

- er see ___ me a - gain. ___

USNAVI:

Damn, we on - ly jok - in', stay broke ___ then.

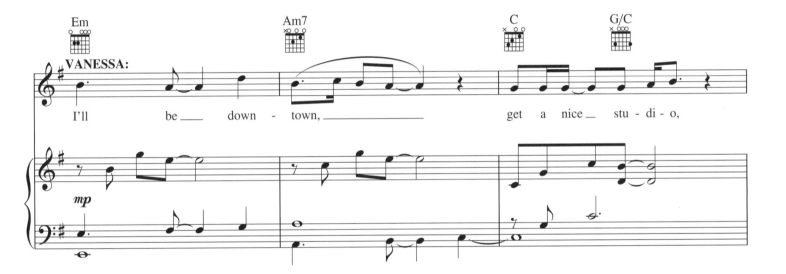

VANESSA:

I'll be ___ down - town, _____ get a nice ___ stu - di - o,

get out of ___ the bar - ri - o. _____ If I win ___ the lot -

BENNY:

For real ___ though, i - mag - ine how it would feel ___ go - in' real ___

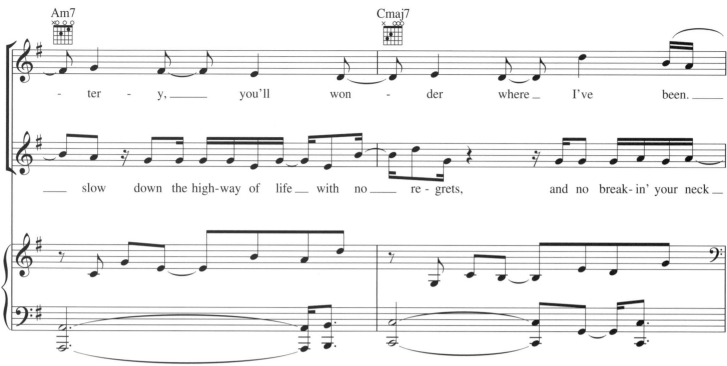

-ter - y, ___ you'll won - der where __ I've been. ___

__ slow down the high-way of life __ with no __ re - grets, and no break-in' your neck __

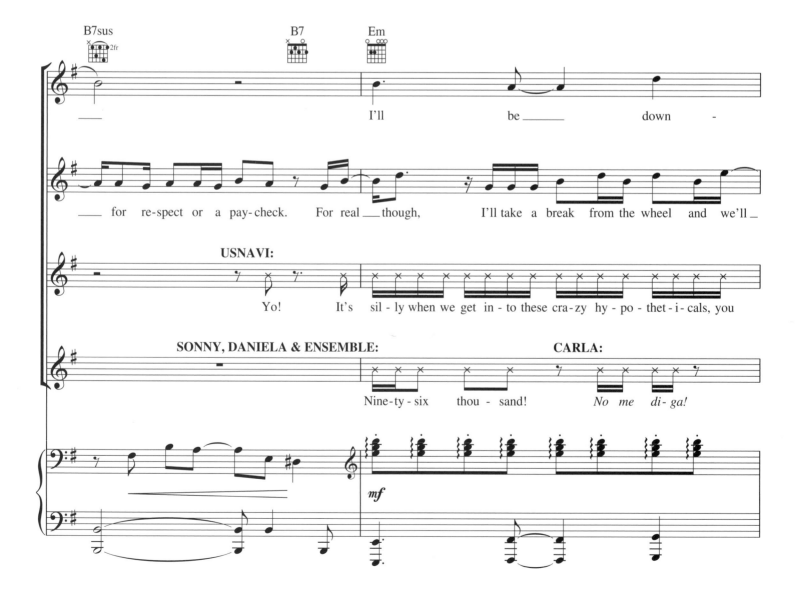

__ for re-spect or a pay-check. For real __ though, I'll take a break from the wheel and we'll __

I'll be ___ down -

USNAVI:

Yo! It's sil - ly when we get in - to these cra-zy hy - po - thet - i - cals, you

SONNY, DANIELA & ENSEMBLE: **CARLA:**

Nine-ty - six thou - sand! *No me di - ga!*

mf

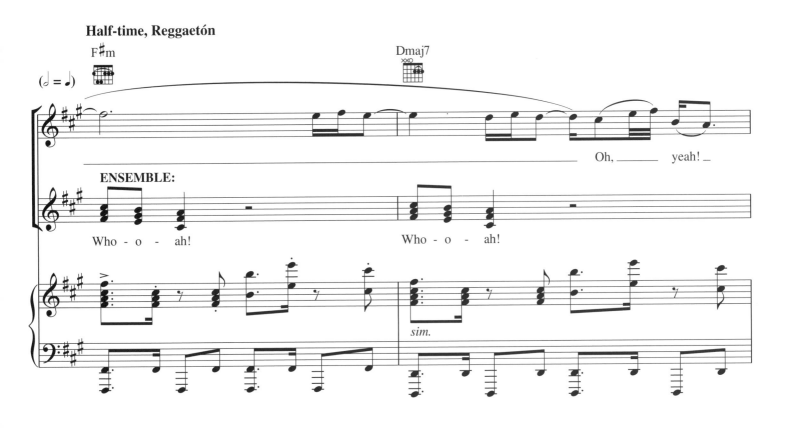

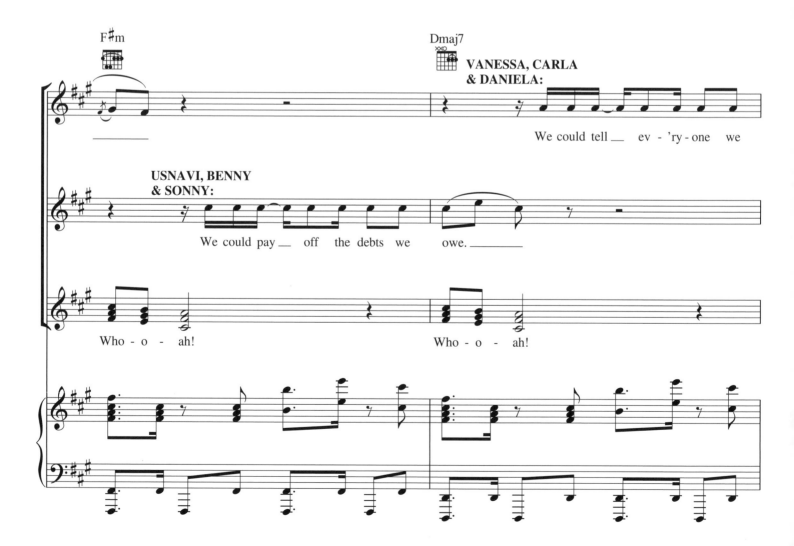

Double-time, Dance-Hall Reggae

-ty - six thou - sand!   Nine - ty - six thou - sand!

We'll __ get the dough __ an'   once __

sim. (both hands)

Nine - ty - six thou - sand!

ALL:

__ we get go - in',   We'll __ get the dough, __ an' once __

fp   *cresc.*

__ we get go - in', we're __ nev - er gon - na stop!

ff   N.C.

8vb

PACIENCIA Y FE

Music and Lyrics by LIN-MANUEL MIRANDA
Arrangement by ALEX LACAMOIRE
and BILL SHERMAN

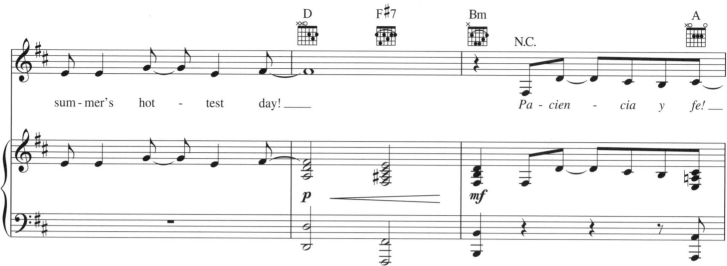

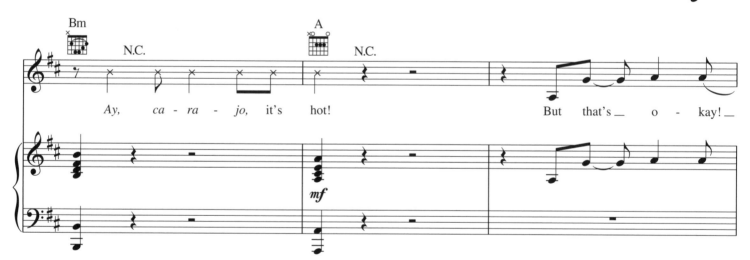

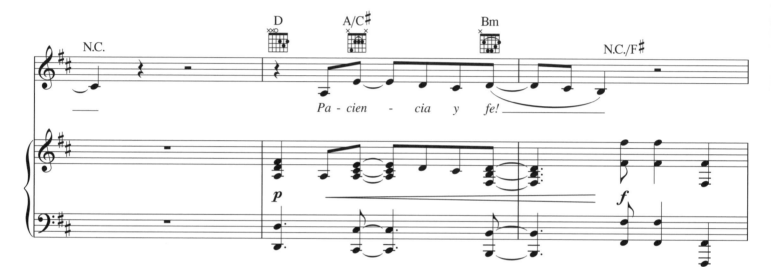

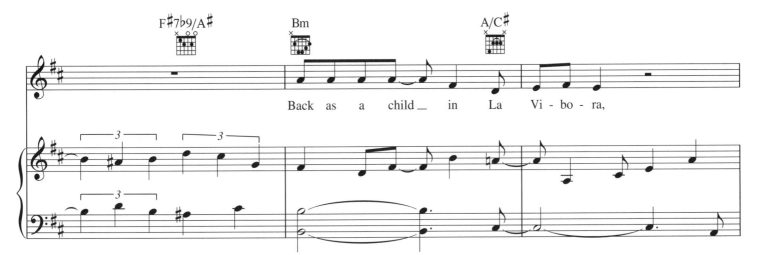

I chased the birds in the pla - za, ___ pray - ing, Ma - má, you would

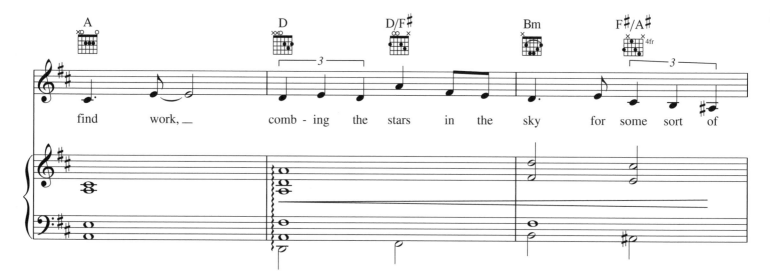

find work, ___ comb - ing the stars in the sky for some sort of

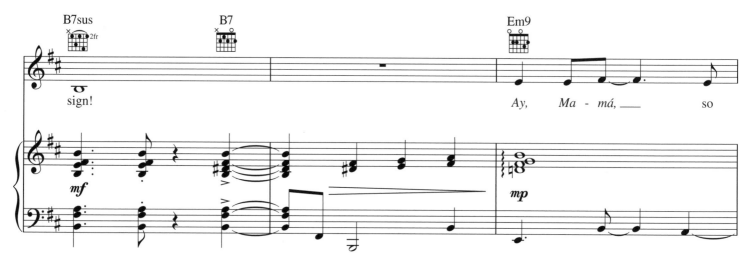

sign! Ay, Ma - má, ___ so

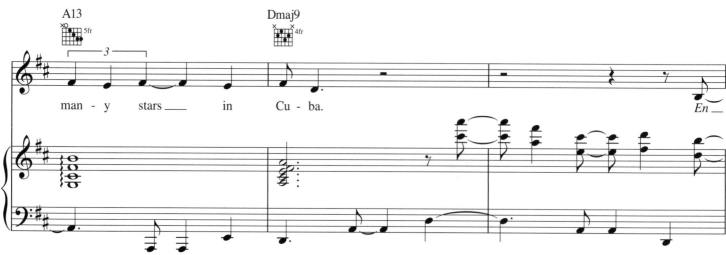

man - y stars ___ in Cu - ba.

En ___

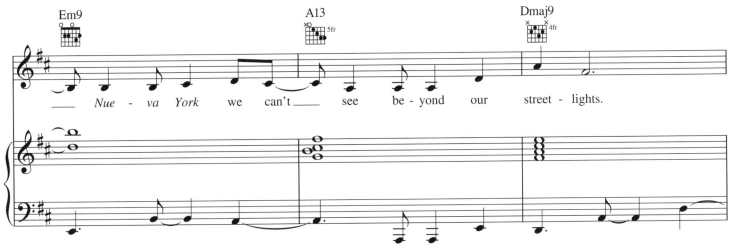

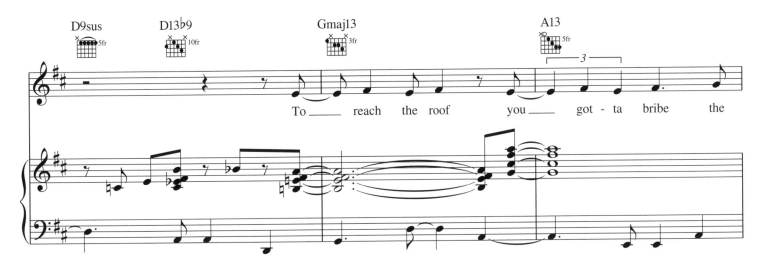

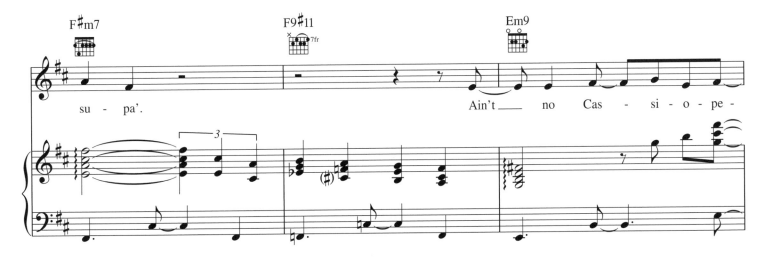

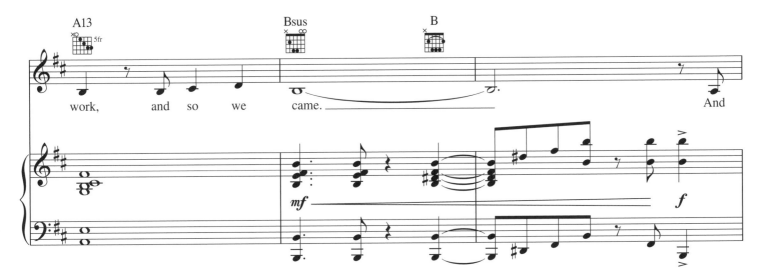

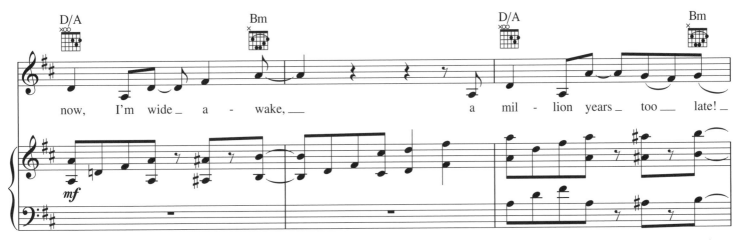

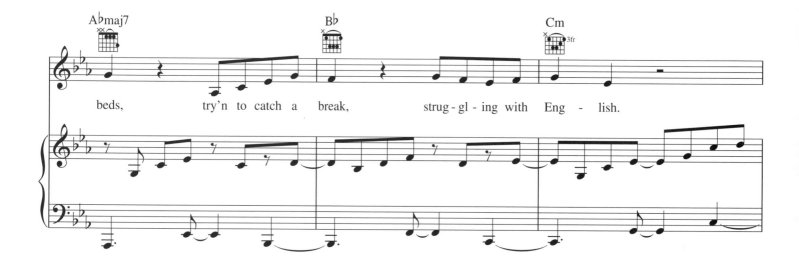

So we cleaned some homes, pol - ish - ing with

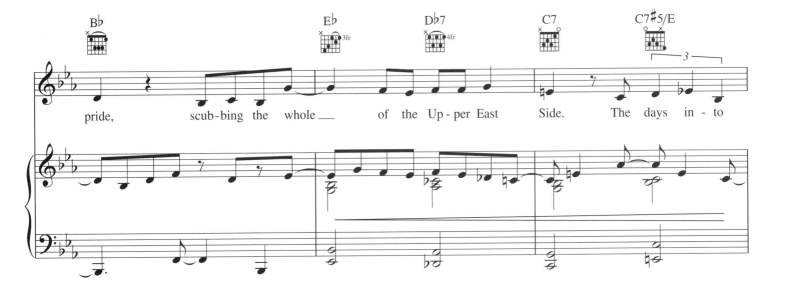

pride, scub-bing the whole __ of the Up - per East Side. The days in - to

weeks, the weeks in - to years and here I stayed. __

ENSEMBLE (Basses):

Pa - cien - cia y fe! __

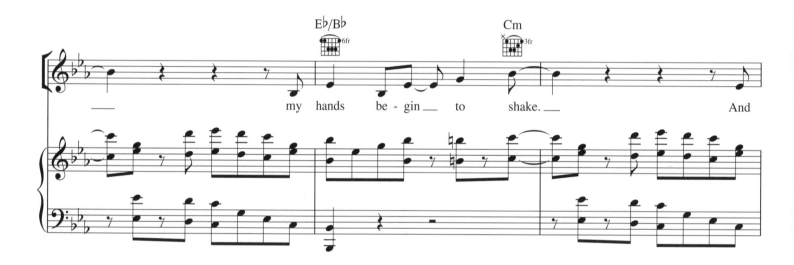

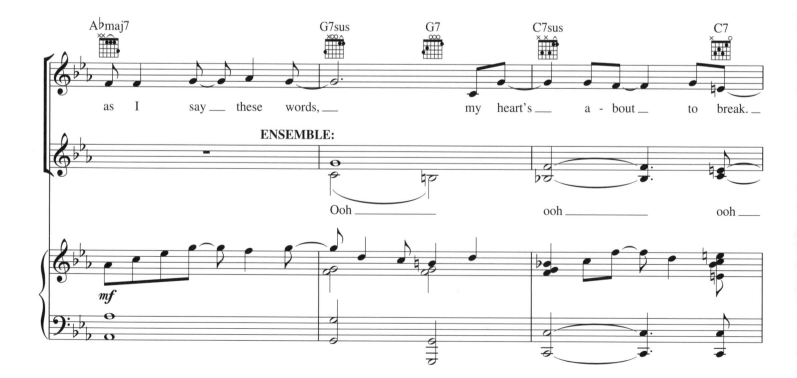

Freely

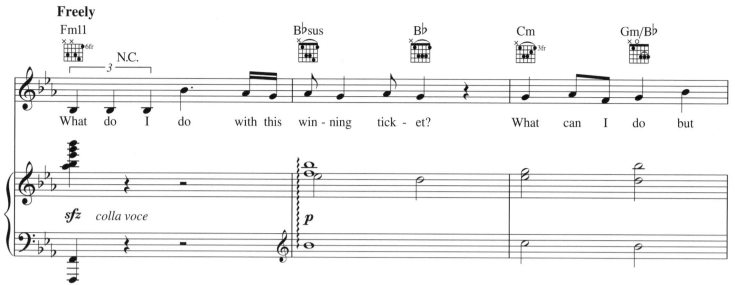

What do I do with this win-ning tick-et? What can I do but

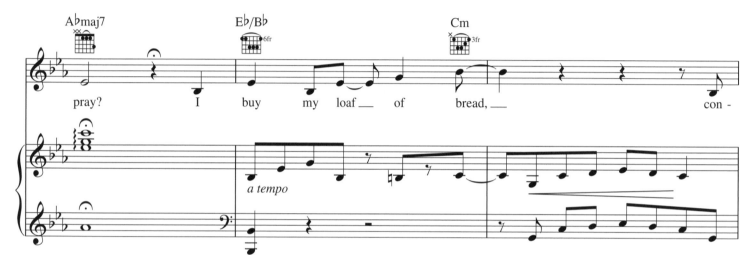

pray? I buy my loaf __ of bread, __ con-

tin - ue with __ my __ day. __ And see you in __ my head, __

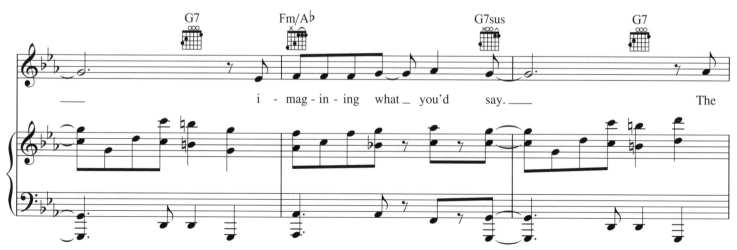

i - mag-in-ing what __ you'd say. __ The

birds, they fly___ a - way.___ Do they fly to La Vi - bo - ra?___

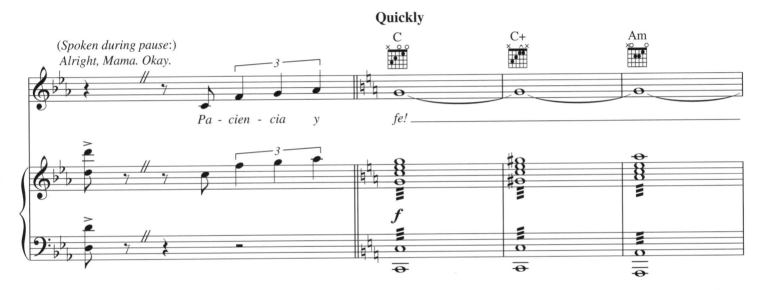

(Spoken during pause:)
Alright, Mama. Okay.

Pa - cien - cia y fe!___

ENSEMBLE:

Ca - lor, ca - lor, ca - lor!

WHEN YOU'RE HOME

Music and Lyrics by LIN-MANUEL MIRANDA
Arrangement by ALEX LACAMOIRE
and BILL SHERMAN

Gently

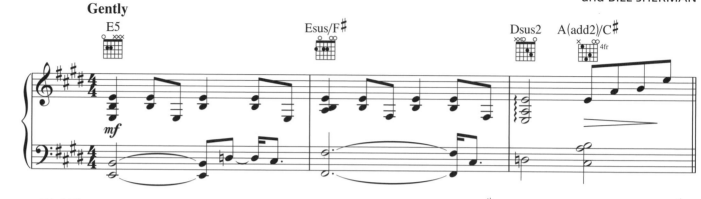

NINA: I used to think _ we lived _ at the top _ of the world, _

_ when the world was just a sub-way map. _ And the

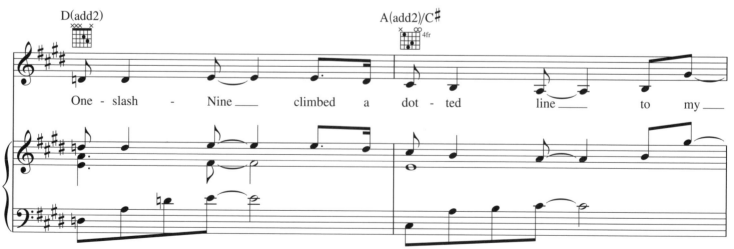

One-slash-Nine _ climbed a dot-ted line _ to my _

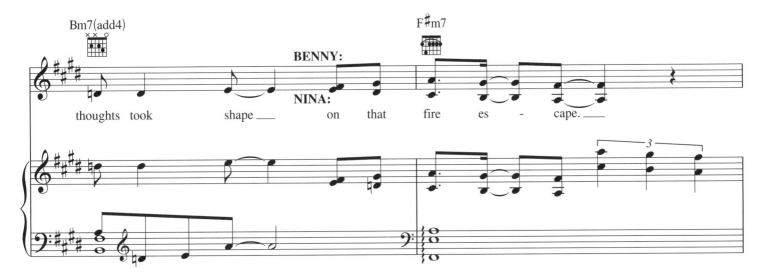

NINA:
Can you __ re-mind __ me of what __ it was like __

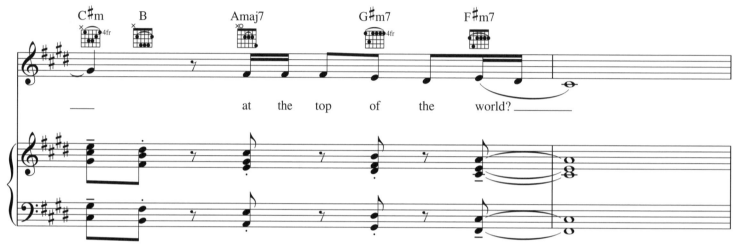

__ at the top of the world? _____

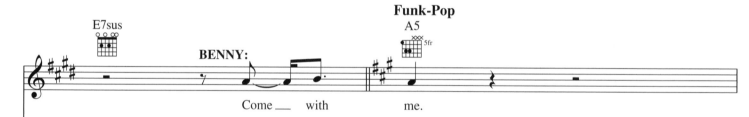

Funk-Pop

BENNY:
Come __ with me.

We be-gin Ju-ly __ with a stop at my __

ran __ like __ hell! __ To your __ fa-ther's dis-patch win - dow, "Hey, let __ me in, __

__ I re-mem - ber __ well! __

NINA:

__ yo! They're com-ing to get me!" You were al - ways in con - stant trou -

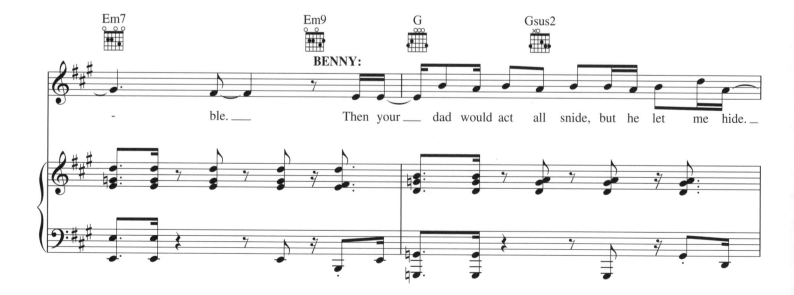

BENNY:

- ble. __ Then your __ dad would act all snide, but he let me hide. __

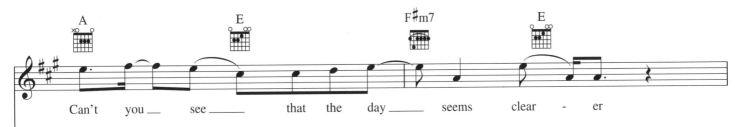

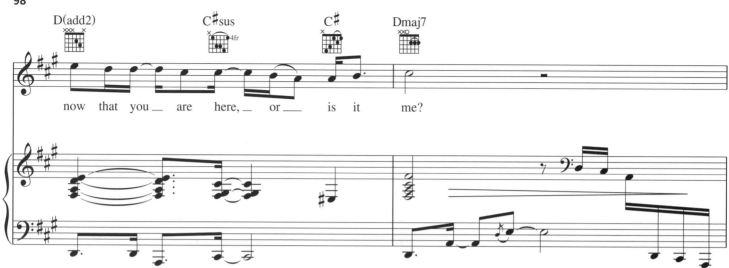

now that you __ are here, __ or __ is it me?

May-be it's just me. ___ We got-ta go, I wan-na show you all I __ know.

The sun is set-ting and the light is get-ting __ low.

NINA:

Are we go-ing to Cas-tle Gar-

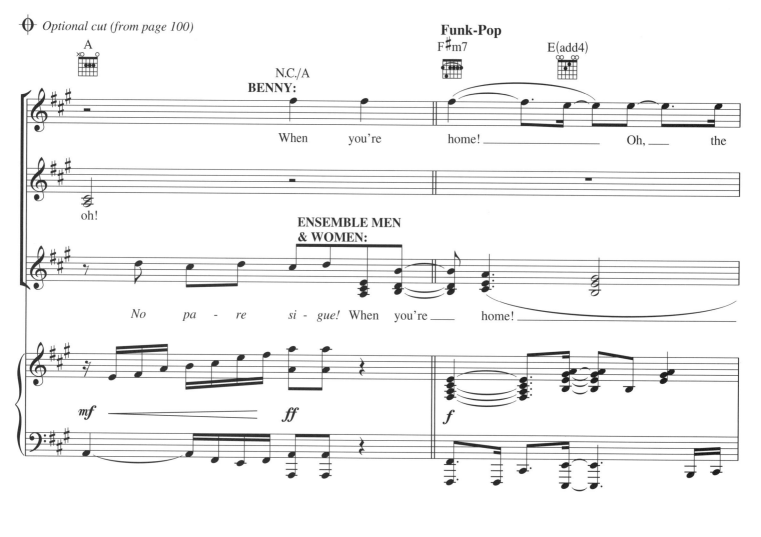

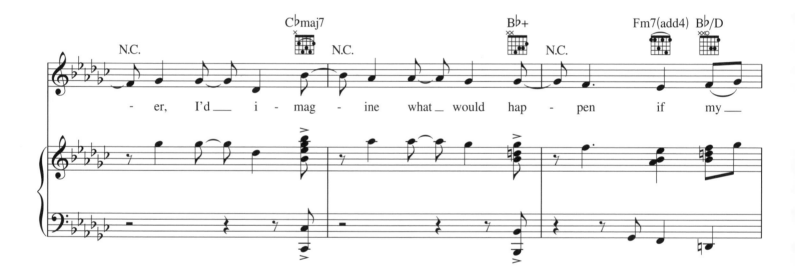

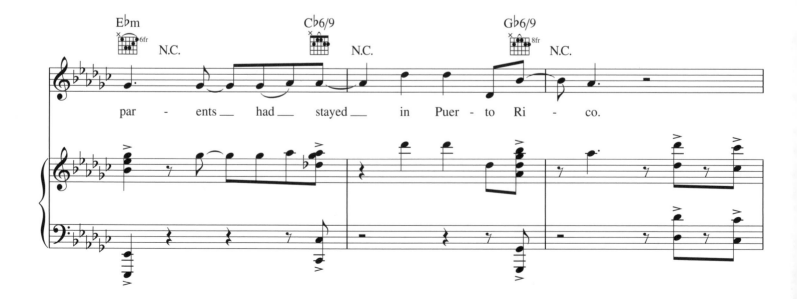

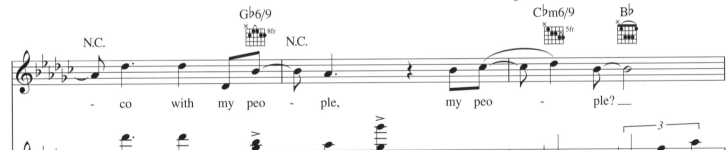

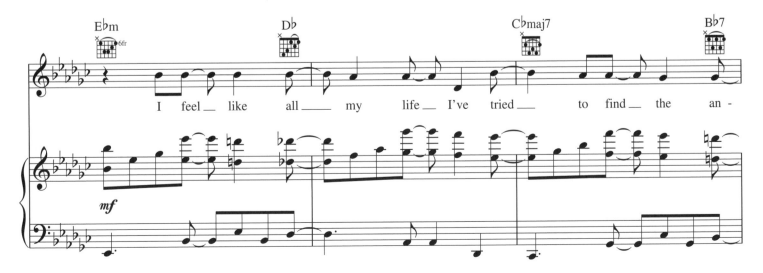

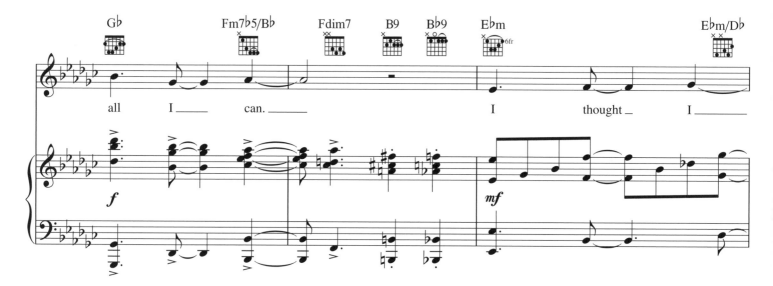

where'm I s'pposed to be? ___ So please don't say you're proud ___ of me when I've

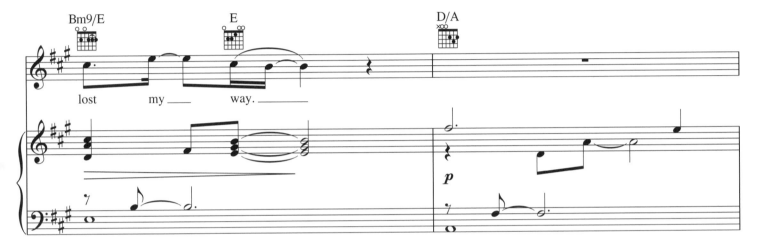

lost my ___ way. ___

BENNY: Then can I say, I

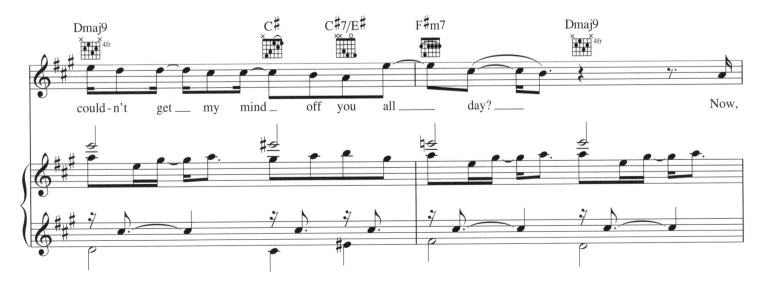

could-n't get ___ my mind ___ off you all ___ day? ___ Now,

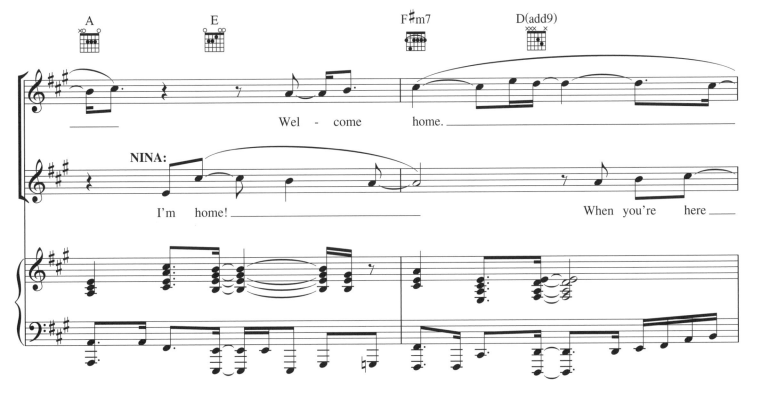

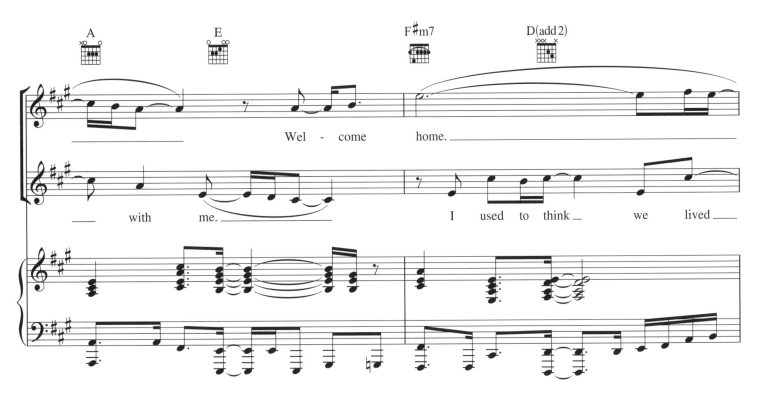

PIRAGUA

Music and Lyrics by LIN-MANUEL MIRANDA
Arrangement by ALEX LACAMOIRE
and BILL SHERMAN

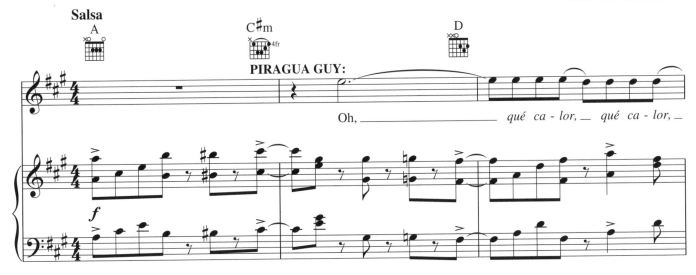

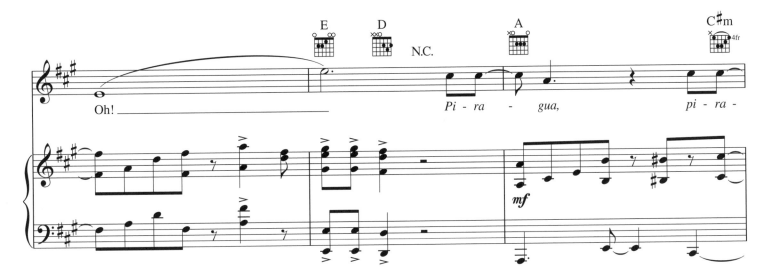

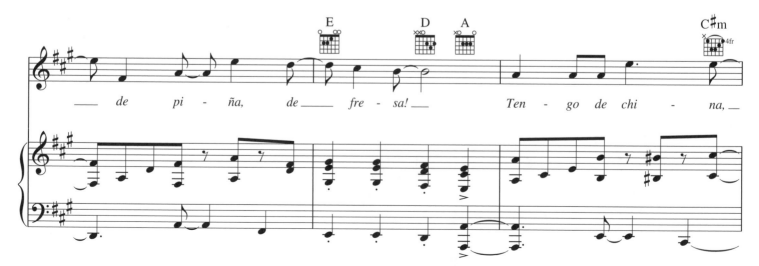

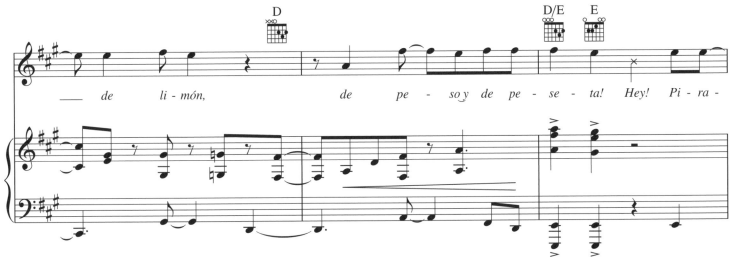

de li - món, de pe - so y de pe - se - ta! Hey! Pi - ra -

- gua, _____ pi - ra - gua! New ___ block of ice, pi - ra -

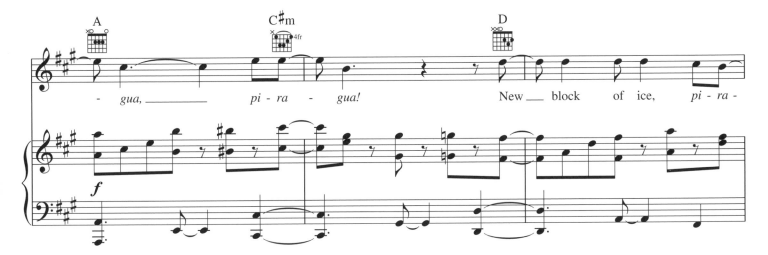

- gua! _____ Pi - ra - gua! pi - ra - gua! So ___

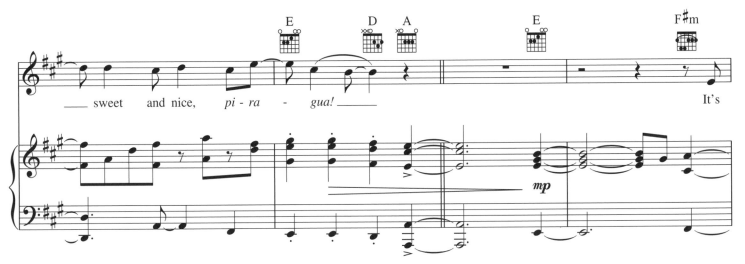

___ sweet and nice, pi - ra - gua! _____ It's

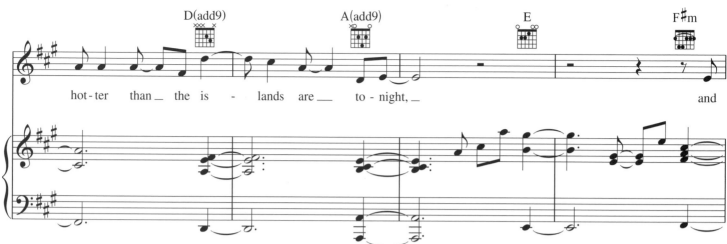

hot-ter than the is - lands are to-night, and

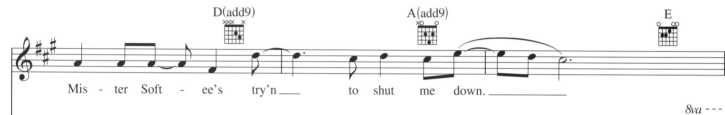

Mis - ter Soft - ee's try'n to shut me down.

But I keep scrap - ing by the fad - ing

light. Hey 'pa - na, this is my town! Pi - ra -

gua, _____ pi - ra - gua! Keep _ scrap - ing by, pi - ra -

- gua! _____ Pi - ra - gua! _____ pi - ra - gua! _____ Keep _

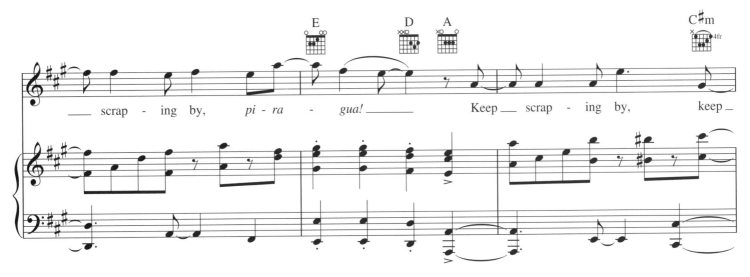

_____ scrap - ing by, pi - ra - gua! _____ Keep _ scrap - ing by, keep _

_____ scrap - ing by! Lai ___ lo le lo lai! Lai ___ lo le lo lai! Keep _

scrap - ing by, keep __ scrap - ing by! *Lai __ lo le lo lai!*

Keep scrap - ing by! _____

Oh, _____ *qué ca - lor, __ qué ca - lor, __*

__ qué ca - lor, __ qué ca - lor! _____

SUNRISE

Music and Lyrics by LIN-MANUEL MIRANDA
Arrangement by ALEX LACAMOIRE
and BILL SHERMAN

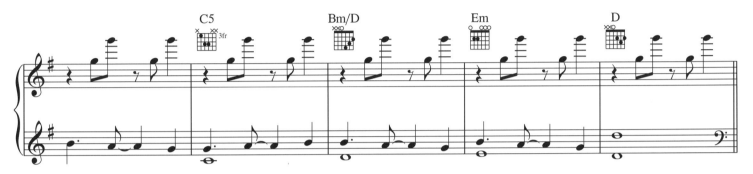

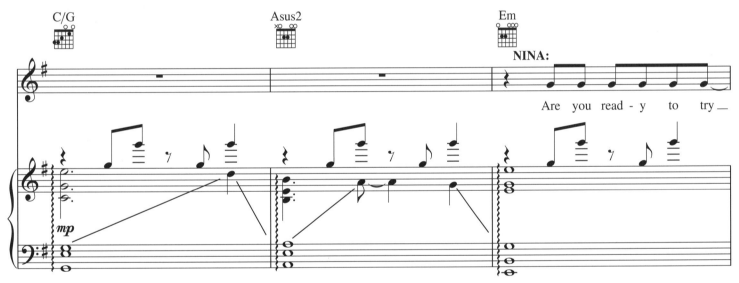

NINA: Are you read-y to try __ a-gain?

BENNY: I think __ I'm read-y.

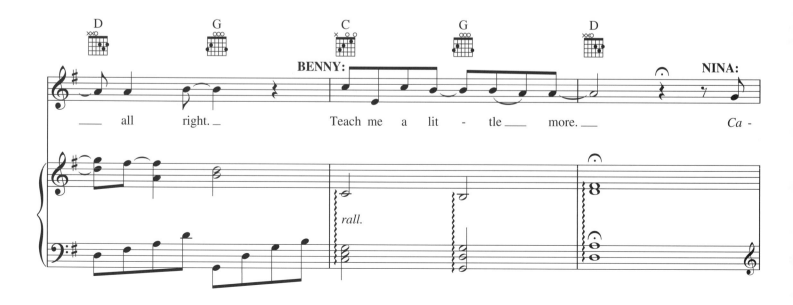

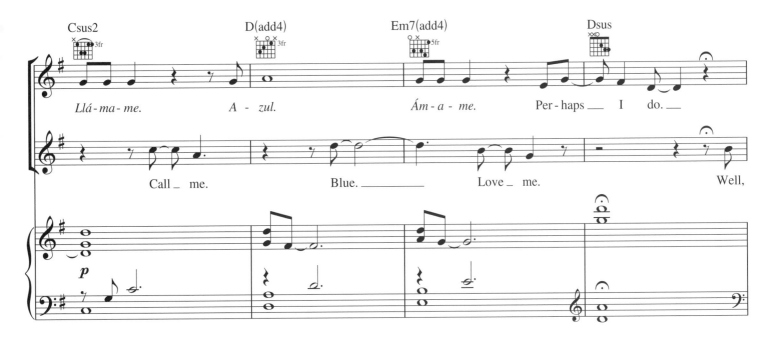

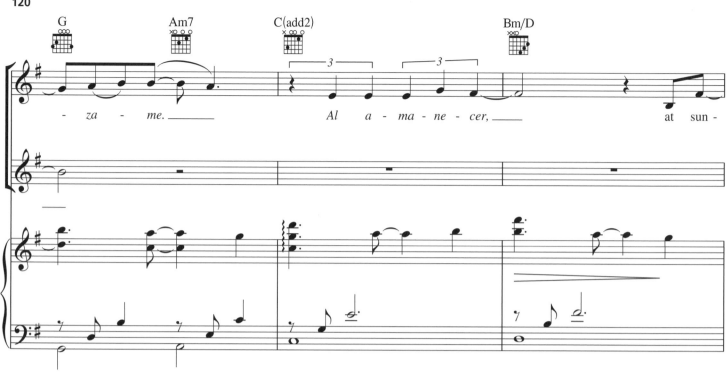

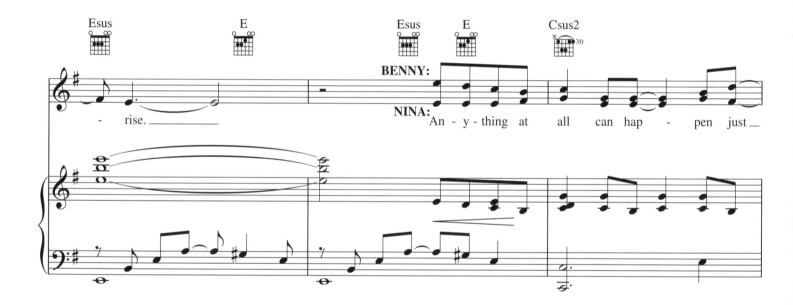

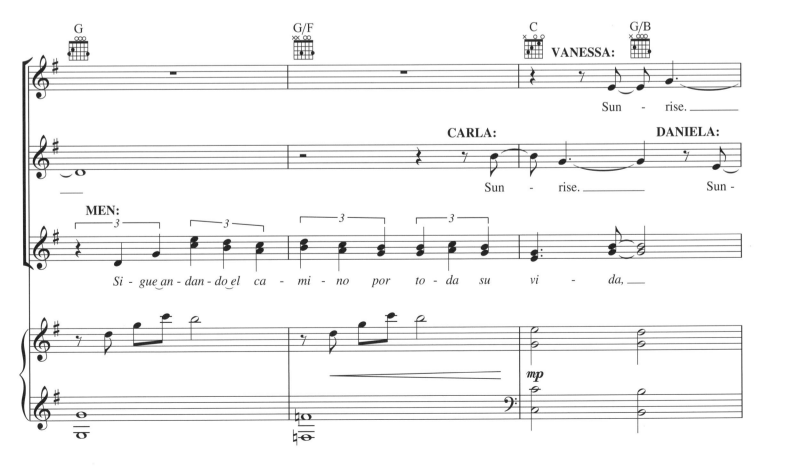

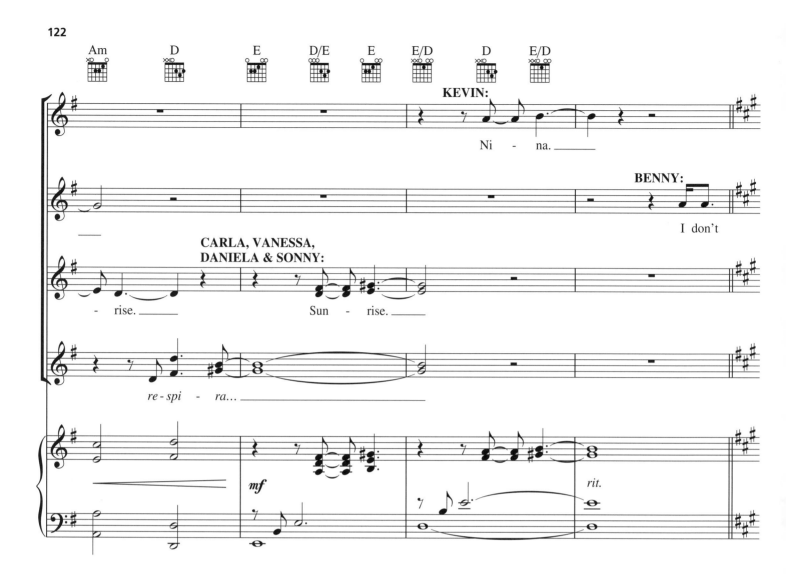

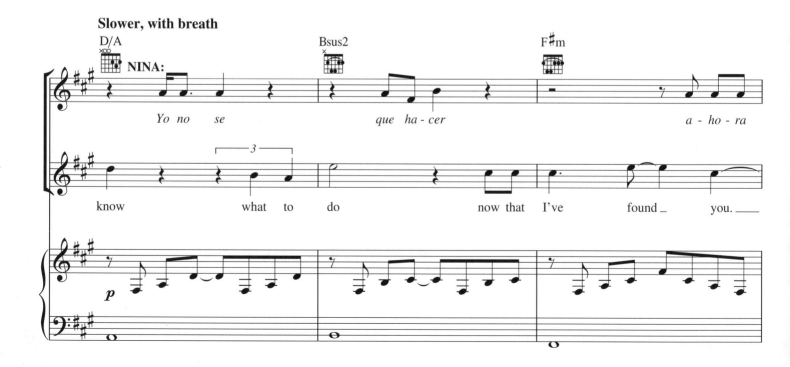

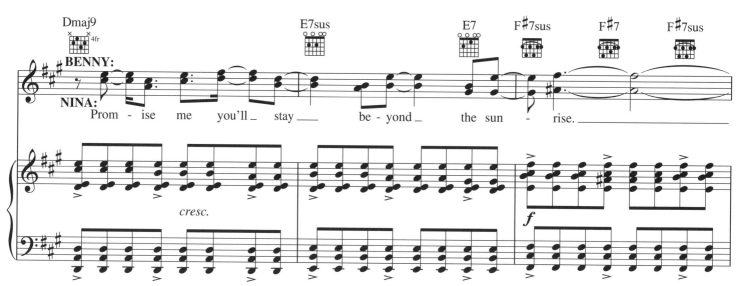

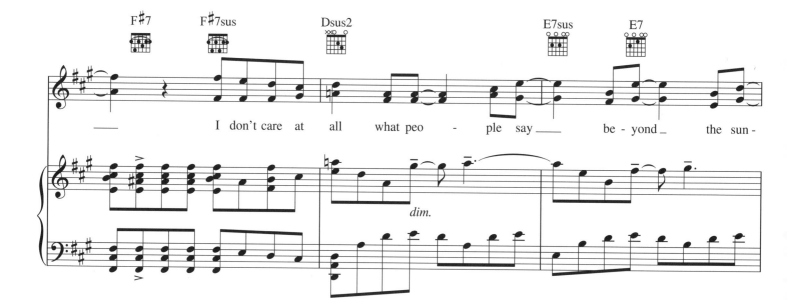

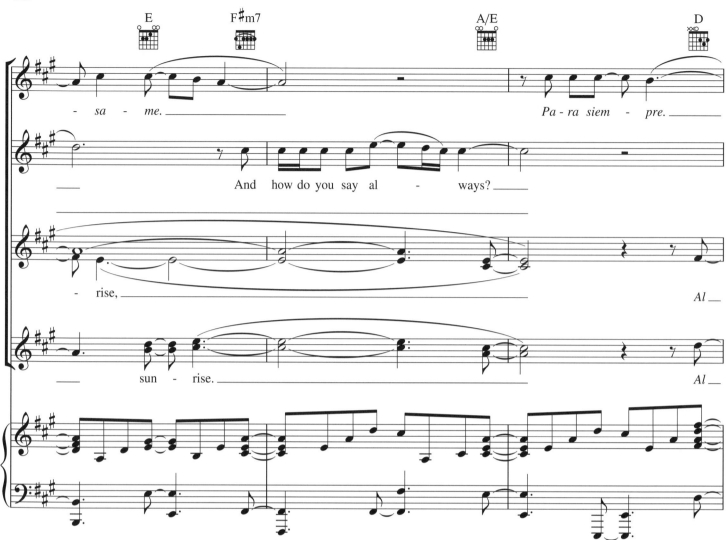

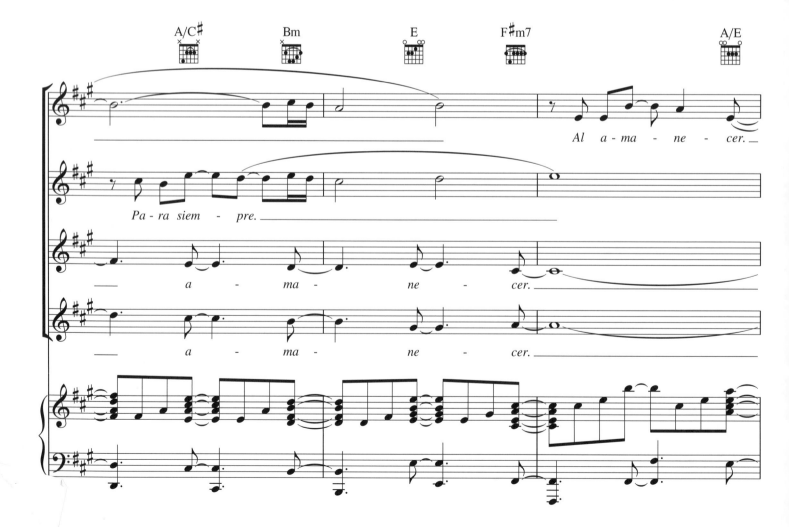

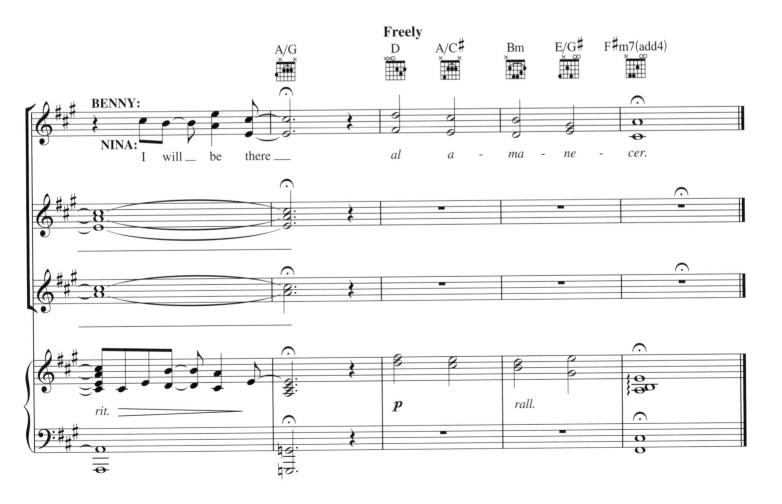

HUNDREDS OF STORIES

Music and Lyrics by LIN-MANUEL MIRANDA
Arrangement by ALEX LACAMOIRE
and BILL SHERMAN

And with our share of the mon-ey, and with our share

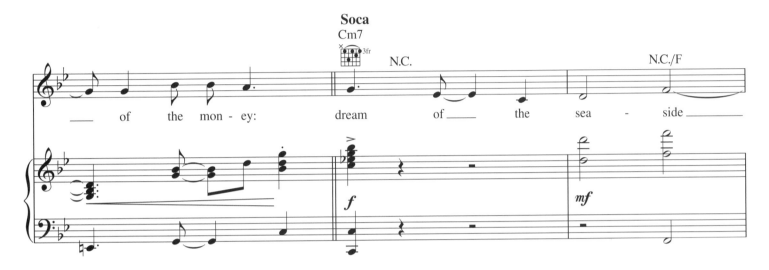

Soca

of the mon-ey: dream of the sea-side

air! See me be-

side you there!

Think of ____ the hun - dreds ___ of sto - ries

we will share! You and I! ___

USNAVI:

CLAUDIA: Ay… _____

CLAUDIA:

Now you ___ can sell your _____

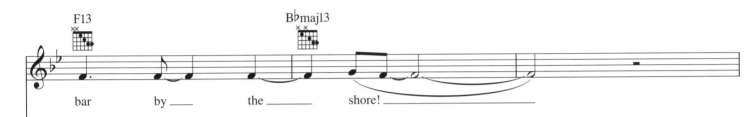

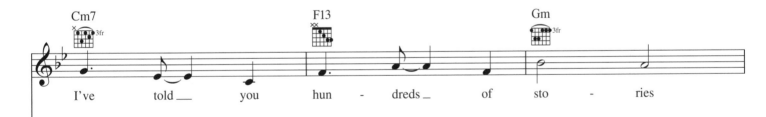

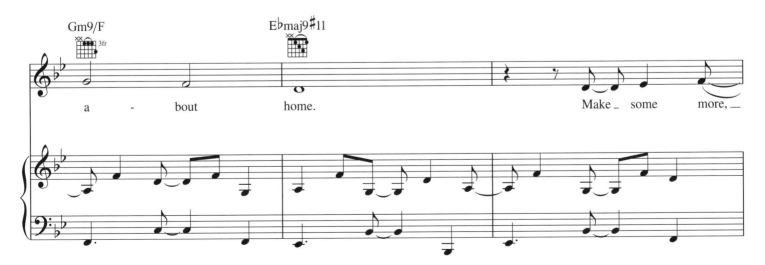

Slower, poco rubato

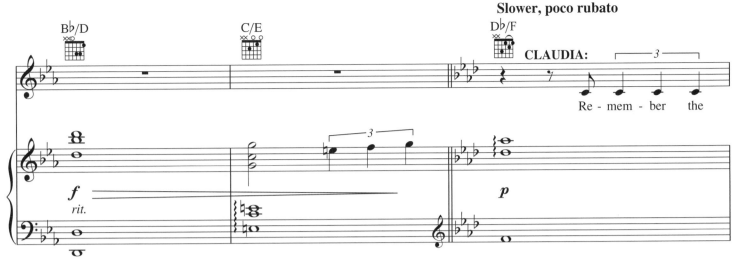

CLAUDIA: Re - mem - ber the

sto - ry of ___ your name.

It was en -

graved on a pass - ing ship ___ on the day ___ your fam - 'ly came. ___

Your fa - ther said, ___ "Us - na - vi, that's

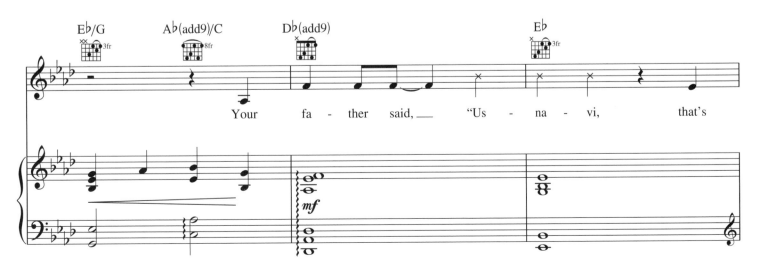

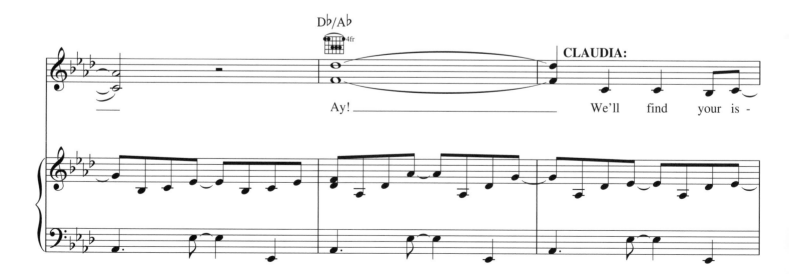

ENOUGH

Music and Lyrics by LIN-MANUEL MIRANDA
Arrangement by ALEX LACAMOIRE
and BILL SHERMAN

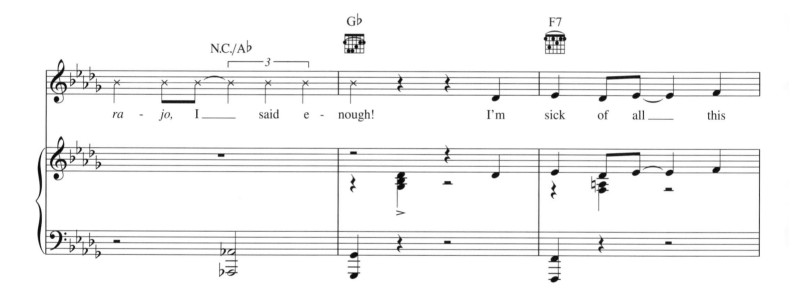

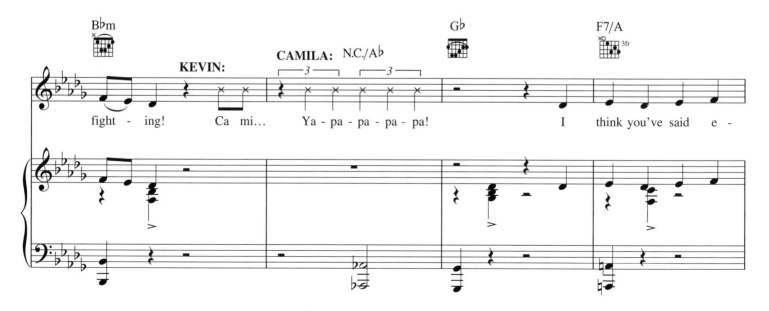

144

148

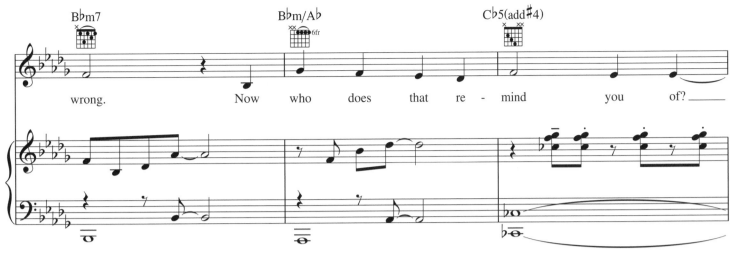

wrong.   Now who does that re - mind   you   of? ___

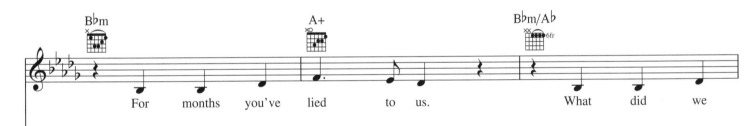

___   You   two ___ de - serve   each   oth - er!

For   months   you've   lied   to   us.   What   did   we

do   to   make   you   think   we   would - n't   do

an-y-thing__ and ev-'ry - thing for you? When you__ have a

prob - lem you come home. You don't run off and

hide from__ your fam - i - ly all __ a - lone! __

You hear me? When you__ have a prob - lem you come

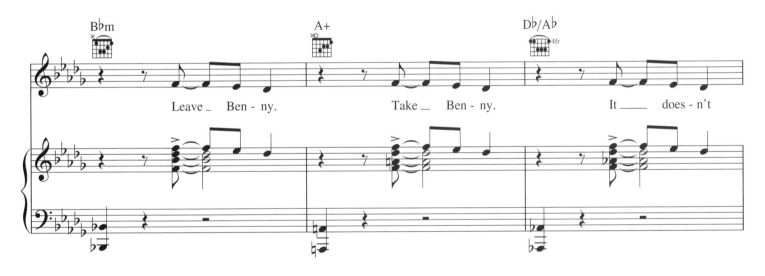

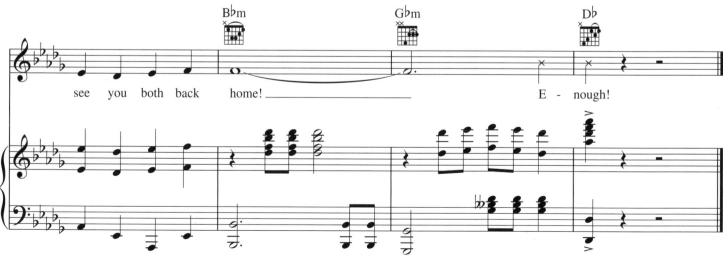

EVERYTHING I KNOW

Music and Lyrics by LIN-MANUEL MIRANDA
Arrangement by ALEX LACAMOIRE
and BILL SHERMAN

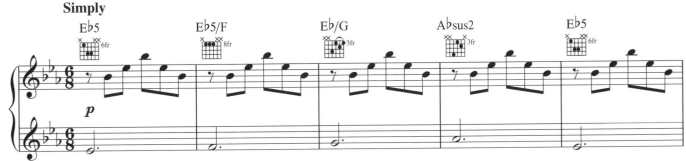

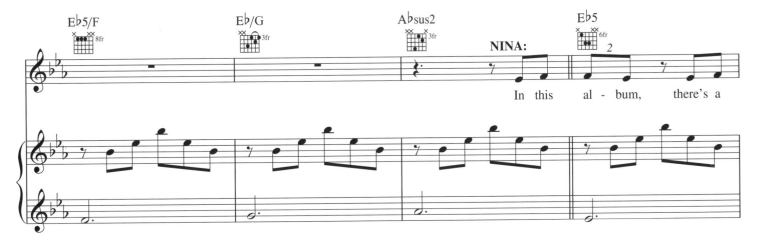

In this al - bum, there's a

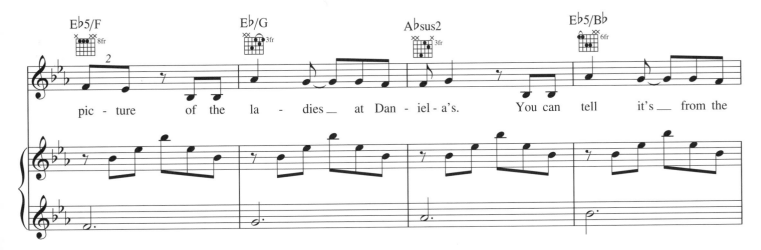

pic - ture of the la - dies __ at Dan - iel - a's. You can tell it's __ from the

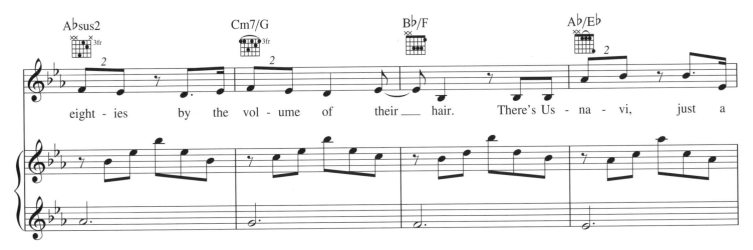

eight - ies by the vol - ume of their __ hair. There's Us - na - vi, just a

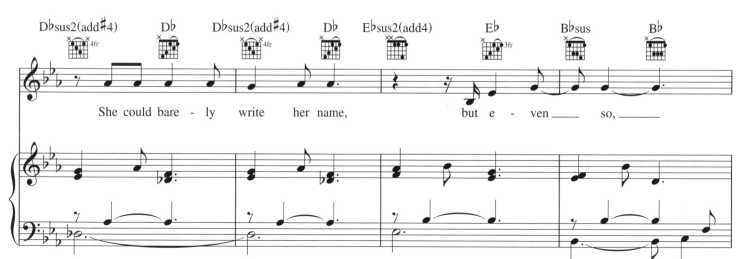

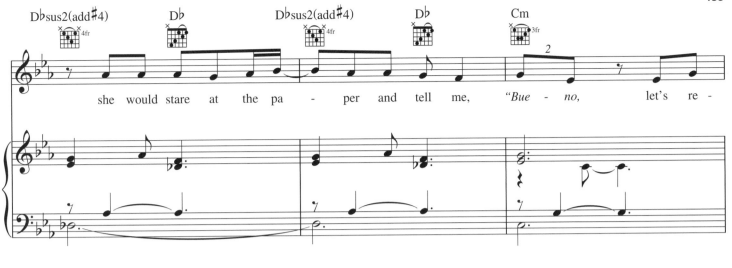

she would stare at the pa - per and tell me, *"Bue - no,* let's re -

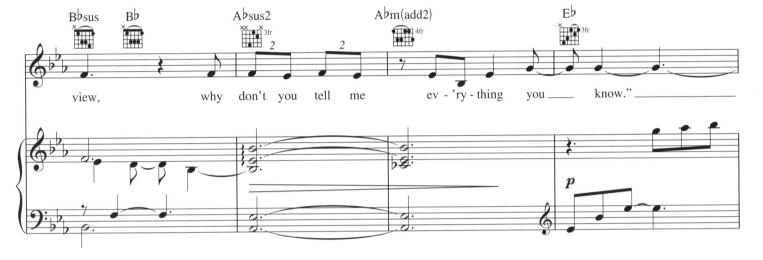

view, why don't you tell me ev - 'ry - thing you ___ know." _____

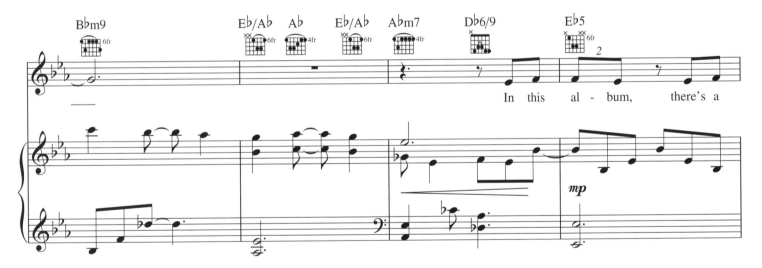

In this al - bum, there's a

pic - ture of A - bue - la ___ in Ha - va - na. She is hold - ing ___ a

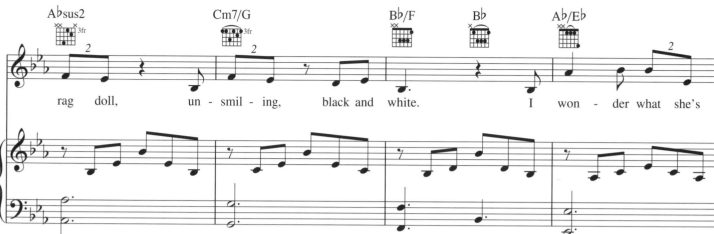

rag doll, un - smil - ing, black and white. I won - der what she's

think - ing. Does she know that she'll be leav - ing _____ for the cit - y on a

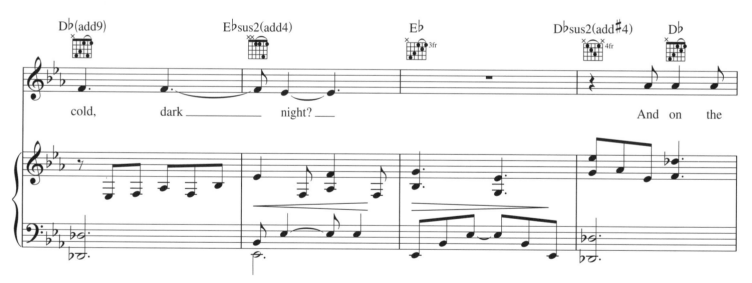

cold, dark _____ night? _____ And on the

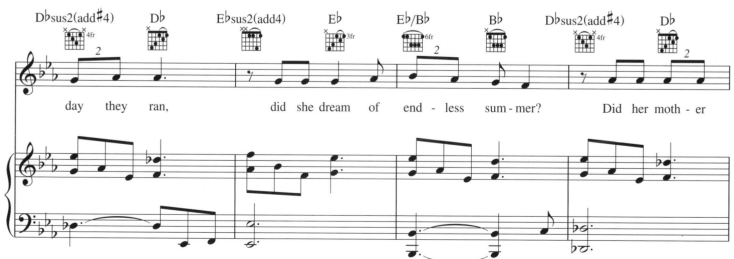

day they ran, did she dream of end - less sum - mer? Did her moth - er

WHEN THE SUN GOES DOWN

Music and Lyrics by LIN-MANUEL MIRANDA
Arrangement by ALEX LACAMOIRE
and BILL SHERMAN

162

* Full palm on black keys